OXFORD
INDIA SHORT
INTRODUCTIONS

PANCHAYATI RAJ

The Oxford India Short
Introductions are concise,
stimulating, and accessible guides
to different aspects of India.
Combining authoritative analysis,
new ideas, and diverse perspectives,
they discuss subjects which are
topical yet enduring, as also
emerging areas of study and debate.

W0235348

OXFORD
INDIA SHORT
INTRODUCTIONS

PANCHAYATI RAJ

KULDEEP MATHUR

OXFORD
UNIVERSITY PRESS

OXFORD
UNIVERSITY PRESS

Oxford University Press is a department of the University of Oxford.
It furthers the University's objective of excellence in research, scholarship,
and education by publishing worldwide. Oxford is a registered trademark of
Oxford University Press in the UK and in certain other countries

Published in India by
Oxford University Press
22 Workspace, 2nd Floor, 1/22 Asaf Ali Road, New Delhi 110002, India

First Edition published in 2013

15th impression 2022

ISBN-13: 978-0-19-809043-4
ISBN-10: 0-19-809043-9

Typeset in 11/15.6 Bembo Std
by Excellent Laser Typesetters, Pitampura, Delhi 110 034
Printed in India by Manipal Technologies Limited, Manipal

For
Anand, Nargis, and Aneesh
who will inherit this world and
make it a better place to live

Contents

7 What does the Future Hold? 133

Boxes and Tables

Boxes

Tables

Preface

There has been a keen interest in the functioning of the Panchayati Raj institutions after they were mandated by the Constitution in 1993. The constitutional step appeared as a triumph for those who believed that this will usher in substantive local democratic governance. Others were sceptical for they thought that rural India was steeped in casteism and traditional paternalistic practices, and will use the panchayats to strengthen their ends.

In the last two decades, there has been a considerable effort from scholars to examine these views on a more empirical basis. Government and policymakers also used this opportunity to learn from experience and made consistent efforts to reform the institutional arrangements to converge with the goals set for them.

When Oxford University Press asked me to contribute on Panchayati Raj in the *Oxford India Short Introductions* series, I accepted the challenging task to review the functioning of the Panchayat institutions and to examine how they are carving out a future for themselves. My thanks to the team at Oxford University Press for giving me this opportunity.

Introduction

Governance, Decentralization, and Panchayati Raj

Panchayati Raj was mandated in the Constitution through the 73rd Amendment in 1993—a time when neo-liberalism was in its ascendancy, with more and more countries getting incorporated in its fold. An important pillar of this ideology was a transformation in the thinking about the role of the state, and a shift in the focus from *government* to *governance*. The forces of globalization and the promotion of a new strategy of development that placed greater reliance on the market and civil society institutions greatly influenced this changed thinking. It came to be believed that the state was the problem and not the solution in improving the delivery of services and eradicating poverty. India accepted this broad perspective when it embarked upon economic reforms in 1991.

Good Governance and New Public Management

This changed thinking was reflected in the way services were delivered to the people. The role and institutional character of the state and the public sector was under pressure to become even more oriented towards the market and the private sector. There was a search for alternative ways of organizing and managing public services, where markets and competition would play a more prominent role, with greater involvement of the private and the voluntary sectors. A new public management movement to reform the public sector sought to incorporate management techniques that reflected the concerns of efficiency which character-ized the market and the private sector. Alternative organizational and implementation strategies were explored relying on the techniques of the for-profit private sector.

At the same time, the discourse on good governance was gaining prominence, and the issue of reforms in policy and in public administration was being raised. The welfare state was being dismantled amid debate on *how much* of the state is necessary. An integral part of this debate concerned the downsizing of the public administration system, and the designing of alternative organizations. Good governance, it was argued, cannot be achieved without efficient and effective public administration and management systems and, equally, public administration and management systems may be ineffective and inefficient in an environment of poor governance characterized by the lack of basic freedoms, lack of respect for the rule of law, and autocratic, idiosyncratic, and unpredictable leadership. Good governance requirements include not only accountability to the public, but also creating an enabling environment for private enterprise and efficient state-operated enterprises (Laribi 1999: 10).

A persuasive contribution influencing the thrust of public sector reforms was that of Osborne and Gaebler (1992) who titled their book *Reinventing Government*, and used the phrase 'entrepreneurial government' to describe the new model of government that they saw emerging in the world. They saw the government's obligation not in providing services, but in seeing that they are provided. A distinction was made between 'steering' and 'rowing', and they argued that governments must confine themselves to giving direction and framing policy while empowering communities to serve themselves.

Decentralization as Devolution

Accountability and community empowerment were the key elements in the new reform strategies, and these crystallized into the concept of decentralization that was promoted enthusiastically in the new public management reforms package. This reforms package offered a menu of choices in decentralizing the delivery of services. The goal was 'de-bureaucratization' and downsizing of the bureaucracy. In keeping accountability and empowerment as the building blocks of new institutions, the effort was to create autonomous institutions and community-based organizations. The autonomous institutions, also known as 'Special Purpose Vehicles' in India, are agencies created to provide a specific service to a specified group of beneficiaries. These agencies are accountable to the stakeholders and, being market-oriented, charge user-costs for the services they provide. It is important to note that these agencies aim at reducing the cost of services, and increasing the effectiveness of the delivery of services. The assumption was that they are more efficient instruments for the delivery of services than large bureaucracies.

Distinct from democratic decentralization that seeks to establish self-government institutions at the local level, this kind of decentralization referred only to the devolution of functions and budgets, and was clearly managerial in content. Political control and democratic accountability were sought to be kept at arm's length for they were the concerns of the 'steering' institutions. Decentralization, understood as devolution, was taken up enthusiastically as a key element of governance reform in most countries of the world. In most economies, the process of learning from the experience of developed countries and bringing about neo-liberal reforms was facilitated by international management consultants under donor-sponsored technical assistance loans (see Laribi 1999 for a review).

Decentralization as devolution was prescribed as a strong tool of development, and for meeting the needs of the poor. This was understood as the delegation of authority to the lower tiers of administrative institutions that could implement programmes for the local people effectively. As the international political climate became more and more preoccupied with neo-liberalism, decentralization also began to be identified with privatization, with a growing belief in the idea that the creation of smaller units in which the government, the private sector, and community organizations participated would be able to produce better results.

The World Bank endorsed this strategy, and promoted the policy of decentralization as a solution to the problem of state institutions being too remote from the daily realities of the lives of the poor. The Bank argues that decentralization can be a powerful tool for achieving development goals in ways that respond to the needs of local communities, by assigning control rights to people who have the information and incentives to make decisions best suited to those needs, and who take responsibility for the political and economic consequences of their decisions. Thus decentralization, here, is not in itself a goal of development, but a means of improving public sector efficiency (World Bank 2000: 106). The emphasis is on efficiency and on remedying the afflictions of the old public administration. To the Bank, decentralization means the formal devolution of power to local decision-makers.

The World Bank and its sister financial agencies have incorporated this prescription in their aid-giving policies, and a large amount of international aid is now being provided to local communities in developing countries, including India, through such decentralized 'autonomous' institutions. Multiple organizations have emerged at the local level. Non-governmental organizations (NGOs) have helped in creating community-based organizations as user committees that manage water supply, sanitation services, and so on. Donor agencies now prefer to provide their assistance through this channel rather than through the government and the formal administrative system, and that is why single purpose agencies that are accountable to the users of services have proliferated at the local level.

Governance Reforms in India

As this neo-liberal scenario was unfolding globally, India also introduced far-reaching changes in its development strategy in 1991. The centrally planned regime was sought to be dismantled, and efforts at opening up the economy and liberalizing it became high on the agenda. Even though the immediate reasons to do so were linked with a severe foreign exchange crisis and the conditions imposed by international institutions in return for giving aid to tide over the crisis, the agenda of economic reform was embedded in the wider neo-liberal discourse of economic development. Emphasis was laid on the notion of governance that encompassed the complementary roles of the state, market, and civil society in social action, where each is in partnership with the others, and all interact to achieve the goals of development and poverty reduction. The definition of governance now moved away from the notion of government, and recognized spheres beyond formal, institutionalized political and administrative structures.

The Eighth Five Year Plan (1992–7), the first to come after India had announced far-reaching changes in its economic policies, signalled a change in the role of the state and the government. It began by acknowledging a considerable backlog in providing for the social consumption needs of the people, particularly the rural population and the urban poor, and, therefore, called for

> ... an innovative approach to development which is based on re-examination and reorientation of the role of the government, the harnessing of the latent energies of the people through their involvement in the process of nation building, and the creation of an environment which encourages people's initiative rather their dependence on the government, and which sets free the forces of growth and modernization.

This reorientation got reflected in the way the government saw how the effective implementation of programmes needed not only the strengthening of its own capacity, but also a new institutional arrangement that involved the people. Subsequent Five Year Plans continued to stress the idea of exploring alternative institutions to provide services to the people.

Constitutional Provision for Panchayats

It must be recognized in the beginning that the impetus for decentralization and instituting panchayats in

India did not come from external sources. It was part of the national aspirations articulated during the freedom struggle led by Mahatma Gandhi. He had an idyllic and romantic view of the village and, in his vision of an independent India, he saw it as the cornerstone of the polity and the economy. There was a long debate at the time of the framing of the Constitution, and the 'modernizers' won the day in rejecting his ideas. However, as a concession, under Article 40 of the Directive Principles of State Policy, the Constitution enjoined the state 'to take steps to organize village panchayats and endow them with such powers and authority as may be necessary to enable them to function as units of self-government'.

While it is true that the panchayats did not emerge out of global pressures, it needs to be recognized that they are embedded in an economy which is rushing to join the globalized world, with a race towards raising the rate of economic growth. The new style of governance is finding ready takers because of a historical legacy of successes in agricultural development in the 1960s and in poverty alleviation interventions through semi-autonomous organizations established at the local level during 1970s, both of which have had a deep impact on Indian public administration. The District Rural Development Agency as a decentralized semi-autonomous institution headed by the district collector has survived in many states despite the introduction of panchayats.

The first steps to establish panchayats were taken in 1957—a response to the recognition that the administration had failed to implement the Community Development Programme, which had been introduced with great fanfare in 1952. But these panchayats were seen as the means to mobilize villagers for the development programmes initiated by the government. When such support was not forthcoming, these panchayats began to be seen as obstacles, and the government went on to strengthen its administrative system and rely on it. There is considerable literature from those days—including government reports—that highlight the continuous conflicts between the panchayat system and the local bureaucracy and political leadership. In most cases, the bureaucracy saw panchayats as encumbrances that had to be tolerated in implementing nationally directed development programmes, while the local political leadership saw them as usurping their power and privileges. Many of the current views on the role and functioning of panchayats can be traced back to the legacy of these early years.

As will be shown later, with the changed political and economic circumstances, panchayats went into decline in the early 1960s, and efforts to revitalize them did not bear fruit for three decades. It was in 1988 that efforts to empower panchayats through a Constitutional Amendment began, which could succeed only in 1993. There was no grassroots movement demanding the installation of panchayats; their establishment reflected the decision of the national elites and policymakers.

However, in framing the constitutional provision, the national policymakers could not carry the state-level and local political leadership with them, and the amendment could not achieve its goal of establishing local self-government. As it happened, while the formal structure of the panchayats was constitutionally mandated, it was left to the states to decide which subjects listed in the Eleventh Schedule would be devolved to them. The states did not go along with the spirit of the Constitution in creating institutions of local self-government, and, consequently, the panchayats continue to suffer from this inadequacy.

Clearly, the picture of the panchayats that emerges is one of reluctant institutions of self-government, fulfilling the formal requirements of the Constitutional Amendment, but hesitant in taking further steps. This weakness in design is compounded by the lack of willingness of the central leadership in amending national laws that impinge on the subjects that were sought to be allocated to the panchayats in the Eleventh Schedule. Many such laws—for example, in the areas of land acquisition, forest management, and watershed development—come into conflict with the powers of the panchayats. In addition, the central government has not hesitated to continue with centrally sponsored schemes that overlap with panchayat functions. With separate budgets and implementing agencies, these schemes demand only support from the panchayats.

Thus, the constitutional framework itself has led to many problems that panchayats have faced in the two decades of their existence. The experience of panchayats in this period has also been greatly influenced by the changed understanding of the role of state in a neo-liberal and globalized scenario in which decentralization is understood more in the language of management than that of democracy. The march of industrialization through the strategy of support to large corporate houses has meant great pressure on the local people to put aside local resources for industrial use rather than for local benefits. This has also seriously constrained the ability of the panchayats to act as units of self-government.

Challenges Facing Panchayats

Panchayats face two types of challenges. The first is at the broader conceptual level. Together with the demand for making the public sector more efficient through the adoption of managerial techniques prevalent in the for-profit private sector, good governance saw decentralization as a method of breaking down a centralized public delivery system into smaller units to make them more responsive to the people that they served. The government's obligation was not in providing services, but in seeing that they are provided. Consequently, alternative organizations and institutions began to be explored. These alternatives were laid out in terms of de-concentration, creating semi-autonomous institutions, privatization, and entering into partnership with community-based organizations or the private sector. The needs of democracy were served by making such institutions accountable to the people that they served. At the policy level, this meant the entry of multifaceted institutions at the local level providing services to specific groups.

From the constitutional point of view, democratic decentralization has meant looking at panchayats as self-governing institutions. Article 40 of the Constitution, which enshrines one of the Directive Principles of State Policy, lays down that the state shall take steps to organize village panchayats, and endow them with such powers and authority as may be necessary to enable them to function as units of self-government. The 73rd Amendment was a step in that direction. The panchayats were to be empowered to develop socio-economic plans of development, and implement them. They were elected by the people and were created as institutions of local democracy.

Both decentralization and democracy take a different meaning in the two conceptualizations. But the result is that governance at the local level has got fragmented, with panchayats having little to do with the setting up of alternative institutions, however democratic.

The second kind of challenge faced by the panchayats is from the social–political dispensation of each state. To a great extent, the empowerment of panchayats has depended on the way the state political leadership has perceived them: as instruments to achieve their own goals of gaining legitimacy and political strength. The fortunes of panchayats have waxed and waned accordingly. Human development indicators—particularly those of literacy and education—have also played significant roles in the variations in the functioning of panchayats across states.

This book seeks to address some of the challenges faced by panchayats in achieving the goals of self-governing institutions. While some of the challenges emanate from the wider changes being effected globally, there are others that stem from the social and economic context of the country. The way these challenges have been met differs widely across the country, and it is difficult to draw a single picture of the experience. The experience of panchayat institutions established after the amendments to the Constitution in 1993, and how they have fared in meeting the objectives set for them, will be explored in the subsequent chapters.

It needs to be emphasized again that there is no single all–India picture. The states have implemented the Constitution Amendment by enacting their own laws and legislative Acts. These may differ from state to state. The states have also differed in the way some of the stipulations have been implemented. However, a broad national picture does emerge and, in the following pages, an attempt is made build to its broad contours.

1

The Gandhian Vision

More than 70 per cent of the people in India live in rural areas. The proportion has come down from around 80 per cent at the time of Indian independence. Poverty has been widespread in rural areas since the colonial times. It has been estimated that around one-third of the Indian population lives below the poverty line, and the majority of this lives in rural areas. According to the Planning Commission, the Scheduled Tribes exhibit the highest level of poverty at 47.4 per cent, followed by the Scheduled Castes at 42.3 per cent, and Other Backward Castes at 31.9 per cent. The dependence of the population on agriculture has been high, and the pressure on agriculture has continued to rise with the increase in population. Moreover, poverty levels differ widely across states (see GoI 2009b and Appendix 2).

The average life expectancy at birth is 63.8 years, but Kerala registers a high of 74 years, and Uttar Pradesh and Madhya Pradesh lows of 60 and 58 years, respectively. According to the 2001 census, the rural female literacy rate was 46.6, with Kerala registering a high of 86.8, and Bihar having a low of 30.1. In terms of years of schooling, there is similar disparity among the states, with Kerala at 6.19 years, while in Bihar, Madhya Pradesh, Andhra Pradesh, and Orissa, it is below 3.5 years. Maternity mortality ratio during 2004–6 has ranged from 95 per 1,000 births to 440 in Uttar Pradesh, 335 in Madhya Pradesh, 388 in Rajasthan, 312 in Bihar, and 480 in Assam.

Two other factors have an important bearing on everyday life in the rural areas. One is that of economic inequality. Agriculture and land-based occupations are the major sources of livelihood for rural people and, thus, ownership of land determines household income to a large extent. Landownership is highly skewed in most states as land reforms have long been scuttled as a political agenda. The Green Revolution of the 1970s saw a significant rise in the proportion of agricultural labourers who owned little or no land, and worked for wages. The relationship between landowners and labourers has been a contentious one, often leading to violence and conflict.

The bitterness in the landowner–labourer relationship is exacerbated by a second factor: social life is still driven by caste-based relationships wherein the upper castes have dominated, and it is they who have cornered most social and economic benefits. Most of the landowners are from the upper castes who command considerable influence in determining the rules and norms of rural society. The lower castes are discriminated against and suppressed in more ways than one, and this is also reflected in their poor human development indicators. Indeed, the lower castes form the bulk of the rural poor. Marginalized and poor, these groups suffer from both social and economic deprivation.

India carries a historical legacy of the neglect of human development indicators, and has suffered from the lack of adequate investment in this sector even after independence. Colonial administrators followed the policy of leaving the villages alone, and extolled the virtues of a *low-need/low-consumption* economy. Not caring for rural India meant the continuous

3

impoverishment of rural areas during colonial rule. The national leadership at the time of independence saw the solution to this problem as lying in modernization and industrialization. This meant the adoption of modern (read Western) institutions in the political realm, and intensive investment in industry to raise the rate of economic growth and so pull India out of poverty. The vision was also one of creating a self-sufficient economy by producing primary products so that the consumer industry could develop.

In Mahatma Gandhi's dream of the country's future, India was seen as a highly decentralized polity, with extensive political and economic autonomy to the villages. The dominant concept was that of *gram swaraj* (village self-rule) envisaging a string of self-sufficient village republics. A web of interdependent political and economic networks through the creation of self-reliant village economies and local self-government was regarded as the most effective way of meeting the basic needs of the people. Gandhi believed that each village must be a complete republic, independent of its neighbours for its vital needs, and yet interdependent for many other needs in which dependence was a necessity. In this structure composed of innumerable

4

villages, there would be ever widening yet ascending circles. He emphasized that life would not be a pyramid, with the apex sustained by the bottom; instead, it would be an oceanic circle whose centre would be the individual, always ready to perish for the village (quoted in Ghosh 2000: 3). Village self-sufficiency meant that, to the maximum extent possible, production was to be based on local resources and conducted close to the location of consumption. Writing during the freedom struggle, Gandhi saw 'a network of such rural organizations (panchayats) functioning in the villages without any connection with the government as the true foundation of civil revolt' (Ibid.). In a sense, he saw them as instruments of mass politics, intended to undermine British authority in rural India, and to become vehicles to usher in an alternative philosophy of political and economic development.

Gandhi's ideas about decentralization and panchayats effectively meant the self-rule of the village community, leaving minimal functions to the governments of the provinces and the Centre. He conceptualized organizing an Indian polity based on communitarian principles in which power does not flow from the top to the bottom, but travels from village communities

5

to the districts, and then upwards to the provinces, and then to the Centre (Bandopadhyay et al. 2003: 3986). Gandhi's panchayats offered an entirely new pattern of structuring the Indian economy and polity which could not fit into the framework of the representative system of parliamentary government and the strategy of economic development associated with it. The Constitution makers did not mention panchayats, neither did they reflect on the philosophy behind its thinking as enunciated by Gandhi. The Constitution took the individual, and not the village, as the basic unit of the political system.

Constitutional Bias towards Centralization

No doubt, there was much appreciation and respect for the Gandhian faith in the village republic, the values of humanitarianism, and non-violence. However, the Constitution that was ultimately adopted was federal and parliamentary in structure, with a pronounced bias towards centralization. Gandhian views were considered outside the realm of practical politics, and were discarded while framing the Constitution. As a concession to the advocates of the panchayat system, the Constitution included the following in its chapter on Directive Principles of State Policy: 'The State shall take steps to organize village panchayats and endow them with such powers and authority as may be necessary to enable them to function as units of self-government.'

Thus, within the Constitution itself, the idea of panchayats becoming building blocks of a new Indian polity was given up. The panchayat system was not accepted as an alternative form of political and economic organization; however, the government was encouraged to organize panchayats within the proposed federal parliamentary structure.

The reasons for this constitutional neglect were embedded in the social context of the time. India had emerged from the traumatic experience of Partition, which had brought untold misery to the people who migrated from one area to another. Also, there were insurrections raising their heads in several parts of the country, and the uppermost concern was to hold the country together. The central political elite perceived that any weakening of the Centre would lead to the unleashing of centrifugal forces that could threaten the very foundations of the new nation. The result was that even the federal system of government that was adopted exhibited a strong bias towards centralization. The Constitution of India made the states deeply dependent on the Centre, if not subordinate to it.

Constituent Assembly Debates

Besides the concern for national unity forming the background of the debates in the Constituent Assembly, the discussions were also marked by issues such as the social and economic exploitation of the depressed classes. Dr B.R. Ambedkar, chairman of the Constitution Drafting Committee, was a powerful voice representing the Scheduled Castes of the country. He had himself experienced hard times facing social discrimination and exploitative practices as he grew up in a village. In response to the Gandhian idealistic view of village life, he argued that village republics were the cause of India's ruination, and empowering village institutions would perpetuate the dominance of the upper castes, who would continue to exploit the lower castes and the poor. He applauded the fact that the draft constitution had 'discarded the village' which he damned as nothing 'but a sink of localism, den of ignorance and narrow-mindedness'.

Within the Constituent Assembly, the omission of the village panchayats as the basis of the new Indian polity was met with emotional and passionate criticism from the Gandhians. A host of distinguished members, including H.V. Kamath, Arum Chandra Guam, T. Prakasam, K. Santhanam, Shebang All Sabena, Alladi Krishnaswamy Ayyar, N.G. Ranga, Mahavir Tyagi, and K.T. Shah, voiced their inability to accept this gross omission. Several resolutions for an amendment were tabled. The following points were recurrently echoed in the debate: (i) Dr Ambedkar's view about village republics was narrow and factually erroneous; (ii) far from villages being the cause of India's ruination, it was the villages that were ruined by colonial exploitation; (iii) the Constituent Assembly engaged in scripting India's Constitution owed its very existence to the rural masses who had contributed principally to the national movement for independence; and (iv) as none of the members of the drafting committee, except one, had participated in the freedom struggle, they were unable to appreciate both the contribution of the rural masses and their potential to transform the country.

However, Dr Ambedkar took a strong stand, and did not even care to reply to the letter dated 10 May 1948 from Dr Rajendra Prasad, the president of the Constituent Assembly, as to why the draft he had circulated did not even use the two words 'Panchayati Raj'. Instead, the reply came four months later (in September 1948) from the secretary of the law ministry, saying that the draft had already been circulated, and that it was far too late to make any changes and if any amendments were desired, the same could be moved on the floor of the House.

What clinched the issue was the intervention of another member of the drafting committee, M. Ananthasayanam Ayyangar, who said,

> ... But as we are situated today, is it at all possible immediately to base our Constitution on village panchayats? I agree that these must be the objective. But where are the republics? They have to be brought into existence ... Therefore, I would advise that in the directives, a clause must be added which insists upon the various governments that may come in the future to establish village panchayats, to give political autonomy, and also economic independence in their

own way to manage their own affairs (Constituent Assembly Debates, 9 November 1948).

Finally, the resolution moved by K. Santhanam was that after Article 31, the following article be added: '31-A. The State shall take steps to organise village panchayats and endow them with such powers and authority as may be necessary to enable them to function as units of self-government.'

The inclusion of panchayats as a Directive Principle of State Policy appeared to be a compromise between the Gandhians and the Ambedkarites. For the promotion of national unity and progressive and just policies, trust was placed on central institutions and not on the democratic strength of the local people. What is significant here is that Nehru remained a silent spectator in the debate.

Gandhi's Followers

Gandhi's concerns about providing self-governing institutions at the village level were kept alive by his faithful followers. The Gandhians organized themselves into a Sarvodaya movement that had Bhoodan (land

11

distribution) as its core element. Acharya Vinobha Bhave, one of the most faithful followers of Gandhi, spearheaded this movement. Between 1951 and 1960, he walked 25,000 miles through the country, persuading 7,00,000 landowners to give up 8 million acres of land to be distributed among the landless.

Jayaprakash Narayan, another leading participant in the nationalist struggle of independence and a Marxist-turned-Gandhian, joined this movement. He argued for the reconstruction of the Indian polity on Gandhian lines, and advocated that the foundation of the polity should be self-governing, self-sufficient, agro-industrial urban-rural communities. The highest political institution should be the *gram sabha*, with the panchayat as its executive. He advocated a *partyless democracy* at the local level. This idea of partyless democracy spearheaded a national debate, and became an issue in the deliberations of many committees that were instituted to explore various forms of Panchayati Raj. These voices became feeble as India went ahead with its centrally directed development programmes. Panchayati Raj came back as part of policy discourse when many programmes faltered at the village level after 1957.

Community Development Programme

The return of Panchayati Raj in 1957 was triggered by the perceived failure of the ambitious Community Development Programme (CDP) begun in 1952. The organizational structure designed to implement this programme was a hierarchical one, with a separate ministry and an extensive bureaucratic structure. Communication and power flowed from the central level to the state level, and then to variegated district administrations for the implementation of the CDP. There was a remarkable expansion in the local bureaucracy which branched into what came to be known as 'developmental bureaucracy' with the district collector assuming the role of district development officer. Under him were the block development officers, extension officers, and village-level workers.

This was the first time that the reach of a centralized bureaucracy touched the village level with a functionary known as the village-level worker. Departmental extension officers were also appointed at the *tehsil* level. The boundaries of tehsils were redrawn to create what came to be known as developmental blocks. A local network of bureaucracy, with links to subject matter

13

departments, was established. The implementation design of the CDP established a hierarchically organized administrative system, with communication links reaching from the village level to the Centre.

Though aimed at eliciting people's participation in development, the programme did not do well. It was realized that the bureaucracy had severe limitations in initiating change and mobilizing people's cooperation. The government appointed a committee, with Balwant Rai Mehta as chairman, to review the entire programme. The recommendations of this committee ushered in the first generation of Panchayati Raj institutions. It has taken long years after this—and many interpretations—before the Constitution was amended in 1993 to include Panchayati Raj as a decentralized institution for local governance.

Concluding Concerns

Two significant issues emerge from the above discussion. One is that the kind of reconstructed polity envisaged by the Gandhians has not been accepted at all. While the Constitution discarded it, there was little appreciation of the idea as the modernizing imperative took over. However, the 'romantic' view of villages projected by the Gandhians has continued to linger, and has informed many public debates exploring the establishment of panchayats. In addition, for many long years, panchayats were advocated to improve central schemes and projects, with the Third Five Year Plan suggesting that the real test 'must be their practical effectiveness as agricultural extension agencies'. It was many years later—around the 1980s—that transformation in these views occurred, and resulted in the 1993 amendment of the Constitution.

The second issue that needs to be underlined is that panchayats were seen as additional institutions for rural development. The government continued to use its own administrative system to implement development programmes and, till today, the panchayats are seen only as supporting instruments in the implementation of programmes decided at the national level. In the quest for efficiency and good management, more often than not, panchayats are seen as obstacles to bureaucratic strategies.

As a consequence, little effort has been made to change the inherited but highly centralized administrative system. The reasoning behind this has been the belief that a strong administration had held the country together during times of crisis—Partition, communal riots, and the process of integrating recalcitrant states—and there is no need to disrupt a system that has stood the test of time. A strong district administration and an all-pervasive civil service, which binds critical administrative positions together and provides leadership in all tasks of the government, have left little scope for thinking about creating new democratic institutions for governance at the local level.

Besides these centralizing features, there has been a pronounced concentration of revenue-raising powers with the Centre. The states were entrusted with functional responsibilities that required large expenditures which could not be met from their own resources. This resulted in large-scale financial transfers from the Centre, designed to meet the requirements of the states. These transfers were undertaken by the Finance Commission, Planning Commission, and various ministries of the Government of India. The panchayats have depended on the states to transfer funds to them. This financial dependency has been accompanied by directions from the Centre to the states detailing what development programmes to choose, and how to implement them.

What needs to be emphasized here is that the persistence of centralizing features in the Indian economy and polity are consequences of the vision of modernization-through-industrialization espoused by the national leadership at the time of independence. This vision is not shared by the Gandhians. However, in deference to the Gandhians, several policies were adopted, and the Directive Principles of State Policy encouraged the state to establish panchayats without making it mandatory. In the overall strategy of development, the Gandhian vision has been a reluctant partner, and there has been a continuous tension between the two.

2

The Journey towards a
Constitutional Mandate

When it became apparent that the bureaucratically organized Community Development Programme (CDP)
was lagging in performance, the Planning Commission
appointed a Study Team led by Balwant Rai Mehta in
1956 to study and report on 'Community Development
Projects and National Extension Service' with a view
to assessing their 'economy and efficiency' and, among
other things, 'the extent to which the movement has
succeeded in utilizing local initiatives and creating institutions to ensure continuity in the process of improving
economic and social conditions in rural areas'. In its
report, the team argued that

> ... community development can only be real when
> the community understands its problems, realizes its

responsibilities, exercises the necessary powers through its chosen representatives, and maintains a constant and intelligent vigilance on local administration.

It concluded that if these programmes were to be effective, there was a need for an agency at the village level, 'which could represent the entire community, assume responsibility, and provide the leadership for implementing development programmes'.

The Study Team then went on to recommend the now well-known three-tier structure of panchayats rising from the village to the district level. In most states, direct elections took place only at the village or panchayat level. The other two institutions—*panchayat samiti* (coinciding with development blocks) and *zilla parishad* (coinciding with the district)—were inter-linked with each other and to the panchayat through indirect elections. Few financial powers were devolved to them, and these institutions were beholden to the district administration for initiating any developmental activity in their area.

Significantly, these Panchayati Raj Institutions (PRIs) were seen as instruments of plan implementation, while politics was perceived as inimical to their effectiveness. Unanimity in elections was construed as an indicator of village consensus and, initially, several state governments offered prizes to those panchayats which elected their leaders unanimously. Efforts to keep politics out found the support of the Gandhians, who emphasized that political parties should find other ways of serving people's interests than by exploiting Panchayati Raj for party ends.

The experience of the initial years—from 1957, when panchayati raj was inaugurated with great fanfare in a district in Rajasthan by Jawaharlal Nehru, to its decline around five years later—belied all expectations, both of the Gandhians and the government. The idealistic picture presented by the Gandhians was considerably blurred and tarnished because the panchayat system brought out into the open the fact that the villages were not conflict-free, but riddled with group rivalry and factionalism. The expectation of a consensual mode of operations was belied as the panchayats provided the means for dominant groups to remain in power.

Those who looked upon PRIs as instruments of development, found, to their dismay, that the leaders were primarily interested in retaining and accumulating power and in distributing patronage, and were often embroiled in political-administrative squabbles and intrigues. Attention was soon diverted from these institutions in the face of more urgent problems stemming from droughts, food crisis, and the Indo-Chinese war.

Increasing agricultural production became an important concern for policymakers as the country faced conditions of food shortage, and they resorted to a bureaucratic strategy in order to meet this challenge. This strategy received considerable sustenance from the recommendations of the Ford Foundation's *Report on India's Food Crisis and Steps to Meet It* (1959: ii) to transform the existing agricultural situation. It said emphatically that '... a far reaching centralized authority with a clear line of command and execution alone can meet the challenge of growing more food ... the administrative structure must be simplified, and clear lines of authority and responsibility established at all levels of government so that policy decisions are carried out at the village level'.

The Period of Decline

The phase of decentralization (beginning 1957) petered out in around five years during which the panchayat system got little support in its role in meeting targets to increase agricultural production. The national policy elites thought that the local political leadership did not reflect the urgency of national demands and, after questioning the role and legitimacy of panchayats in the national crisis, sidelined them in the development effort. From 1962 onwards, panchayats suffered a decline, not only because the CDP, which they were enjoined to help implement, lost its financial support, but also because in the priority of meeting the food crisis, these institutions were not seen as a source of strength and support. However, the neglect of panchayats during the 1964–80 period meant that while the institutions carried on in their organizational form, no elections were held. Those who had been elected continued in their elected positions, exercising whatever power they could in the absence of any financial allocations. A large number of such locally elected leaders emerged who began to link themselves politically with the state leadership by providing them with 'vote banks' in exchange for the freedom to exercise local influence.

During this period, local vote bank politics emerged, encouraging national leaders to cater to those state leaders who had large vote banks behind them. The Congress party was the major beneficiary of this schema, with local leaders ensuring support to the Congress leadership through an intricate system of manipulation and patronage. As the Congress party—the more important national party—began to lose touch with local issues, there emerged 'people-oriented' parties that were regional in nature and responded to sectarian interests. These parties began to assert themselves at the national level also, and ushered in an era of coalition governments.

On the administrative front, the implementation of the new agricultural strategy to increase food production encouraged the feeling that development schemes could be made successful if the central government continued to exercise control over them after promoting them, and also monitor their performance to ensure they adhered to pre-planned guidelines.

During the Fifth Five Year Plan beginning in 1971–2, a spate of schemes were introduced by the central government to alleviate rural poverty. These were implemented at the local level by the states and district administrations, but were planned and financed by the central government, which kept a close watch to see that the implementation did not deviate from pre-set guidelines. The Small Farmers Development Agency, Drought Prone Area Programme, and the Integrated Tribal Development Programme introduced during this time were not located under the zilla parishad. These schemes came to be known as centrally sponsored schemes, and the format continues to be in use today.

In addition, while the funds for the panchayats were dried up, the funds for departments implementing programmes at the local level were augmented. This strengthened the local bureaucracy, which found its own ways to consult the villagers when needed. The local political leadership—with the panchayats neither having funds nor holding elections—found it profitable to link themselves with these bureaucratic functionaries and influence the way in which direct benefits would accrue.

An analysis of the reasons for the decline of the panchayats during this period will remain incomplete unless the characteristics of the weak design of the structure is also emphasized. The panchayat institutions were established under separate Acts legislated by state governments. This meant that the nature of decentralization and its extent varied with the political and administrative interests of each state. Little responsibility for planning and few powers to raise resources were devolved to these institutions. Instead of making them the channels for the activities it planned, the government continued to use its bureaucratic machinery to carry out its own poverty alleviation programmes. Further, the state governments demonstrated their disinterest in these institutions by frequently postponing elections. The leadership, once elected, found such postponements to be in their interest.

It is also important to point out that the panchayats were not seen as institutions of people's participation that played a role in deepening democracy. They were usually perceived as instruments to facilitate the implementation of national policy. Even during the initial years of enthusiasm, their performance was evaluated from their capacity to increase agricultural production. The national leadership perceived the local panchayats as neglecting this primary task and, thus, not reflecting the urgency of national demands. The panchayats were sidelined because they did not appear to be the prime movers of development.

Efforts at Revitalizing the Panchayat

The victory of Janata Party in 1977 marked a return of interest in decentralization and Panchayati Raj. The conglomeration of political parties that had come into power attacked the Indira Gandhi regime as being a highly centralized one, with power concentrated in Delhi. The political climate underwent a change. It signalled the ascendance of a political coalition in which agrarian interests were senior partners. These interests demanded a greater control of resources and more active participation in state politics.

Simultaneously, the new government at the Centre was concerned with issues of the centralization of planning as challenges to the improvement of the country's developmental performance. The Janata Party enunciated a clear statement on decentralization in its Five Year Plan for 1978–83, where it proposed that the Plan would 'require the creation of full time planning machinery at the Block and District levels and will call for great deal more of public participation'(GoI 1978b: 184). It further stated that 'the bulk of investment on agriculture, minor irrigation, animal husbandry, fishing, forestry, marketing or processing cottage and

26

small scale industries including water supply, housing, health, education, sanitation, local transport etc. are clearly amenable to planning at local level' (Ibid.: 188).

In 1977, the Planning Commission appointed a Working Group to prepare guidelines to initiate block-level planning in the country. At the outset itself, the Working Group emphasized that 'the issue whether a district or block is more appropriate for the purpose of planning need not be viewed with rigidity.' (GoI 1978a: 2) It is not an either-or choice for them, and the group viewed block-level planning as an important link in the multi-level planning process. It then went on to recommend the delegation of power to the district level and below, and the creation of planning cells so that professionals could be available.

Together with this initiative, the Government of India appointed another committee to review panchayat institutions (GoI 1978a). Known as the Ashok Mehta Committee, its recommendations sought to evolve an effective Panchayati Raj system, based on the district as the unit of administration and planning. It modified the three-tier system by recommending the *mandal panchayat* as the base unit.

The Ashok Mehta Committee was greatly influenced by the government's aim of decentralizing planning, and saw panchayat institutions as institutions of local-level planning. However, it also saw panchayat institutions as political and administrative units, with a potential of becoming units of local governance in the future. The committee's report pointed out that there was lack of clarity regarding these institutions, with many images existing side-by-side, which tend to militate against each other in the short run. It recommended that the district should be the point of decentralization, and powers of taxation (to raise revenue) should be given to it. It allowed for political parties to function at this level. It did away with the panchayat, and recommended a two-tier system with mandal panchayats in the next tier. However, it appears that the concern for decentralization was technical: the real goal was to improve the planning process and counter the allegation of 'too much planning' from above.

Three state governments—West Bengal, Karnataka, and Andhra Pradesh—responded to the revitalization efforts at the political level. These states were ruled by non-Congress governments, and readily used the opportunity provided by the report to inject new life into PRIs. Regular elections were held, and some powers were devolved to the panchayats and panchayat samitis to perform local functions. However, in both West Bengal and Andhra Pradesh, the motivation behind doing all this was political. The parties that had come to power were attempting to build and widen their support and spheres of influence. Under constant threat from the Centre, they thought that one way to stand up to it was to strengthen local-level institutions.

If the Left parties in West Bengal were attempting to mobilize the rural areas, N.T. Rama Rao, who won the elections on the basis of his charisma in Andhra Pradesh, was in the urgent need of consolidating the influence of his party in the countryside. In none of these states was there an agenda to decentralize governance by allowing the panchayats to develop into powerful and autonomous institutions of self-government (Bandopadhyay 2003: 3987). The Karnataka experiment, however, was hailed as a bold attempt at decentralization. A new form of district administrative system was attempted, and there was even some thinking towards making the district government the third tier in the federal system. But this

29

experiment was short-lived. The party that had initiated this programme lost the elections, and the party voted into power chose to revert to the old system.

In conclusion, it needs to be pointed out that there have been two generations of panchayat institutions in India. Those established following the recommendations of the Balwant Rai Mehta Committee were largely non-political, and were concerned with the implementation of the CDP. The institutions were seen in a purely technical manner; their goal was to help implement a central programme. Once financial support to the central programme weakened, these institutions could not sustain themselves, and the political and administrative leadership asserted itself.

The new panchayats that came into being in Karnataka, West Bengal, and Andhra Pradesh twenty years later, following the recommendations of the Ashok Mehta Committee, derived their motivation from the keenness of the state-level political leaderships to expand their political base in the rural areas. The panchayats of this generation have survived in a state like West Bengal only because the Left Front government continued to be in power (until 2011) since the time they were introduced in 1978–9.

Karnataka was the only state that attempted to change the system of administration to reflect the changes brought about by decentralization through panchayats. However, these efforts were nullified once the Congress party lost power in the state. There was little demand for decentralization or any protest against this move.

At the central government level, the victory of the Janata Party in 1977 brought in a diverse group of people. They had benefited from the new agricultural strategy, and had felt aggrieved by the centralization processes dominant in the earlier regime. The victory marked the ascendance of the political coalition that came into power had influential representation of agrarian interests. Their agenda was to decentralize planning and the implementation processes. At the state level, this coalition demanded more autonomy and resources to control the state's economy. Diverse political parties at the state level hoped to create and use a stronger political base from the rural areas to gain greater leverage with the Centre in wresting greater autonomy. This coalition, paradoxically, stopped at the demands of decentralization for the state-level only; it was reluctant to decentralize further. Again, the Centre intervened to unfold another chapter in the evolution of decentralization practices.

The Third Generation Panchayats

Even after 1980, when the Congress party returned to power, the concern for participative planning continued. In 1982, the Planning Commission brought out a *Working Group Report on District Planning*, and laid considerable stress on people's participation because it was considered necessary 'to reduce the unequal distribution of power in the rural areas'. It went on to express dissatisfaction with existing institutional arrangements of democratic decentralization, seeing them as having 'fallen prey to power manipulation of the rural elite' and giving rise to 'what may be called inner limits to public participation' (GoI 1982). In 1985, another committee of the Planning Commission, set up to review the existing administrative arrangements for rural development and poverty alleviation programmes, submitted its report (GoI 1985). This committee emphasized that various programmes of rural development would become realistic and meaningful only if people's representatives were actively involved in local-level planning, design formulation, implementation of schemes, and selection of beneficiaries in the anti-poverty and employment-generation programmes: 'In order that the felt need of the local people and the area are articulated for planning, and priorities are effectively established and implemented, there is no better instrument to meet this need than the panchayati raj institutions' (Ibid.).

Amendment to the Constitution

With these reports in hand, the then Prime Minister Rajiv Gandhi went about consulting the district collectors at a series of meetings held in Bhopal, Hyderabad, Imphal, Jaipur, and Coimbatore. The government then modelled a bill on the lines that L.M. Singhvi formulated as an Appendix to the Ashok Mehta Committee Report. While accepting the three-tier structure in this report, he had made two strong points: (i) that panchayats should be recognized as self-governing institutions, and (ii) these institutions should be provided by the Constitution. These recommendations were endorsed by the government, and the 64th Amendment Bill on these lines was introduced in the Lok Sabha in 1989.

However, the bill was defeated in the Rajya Sabha. Opposition to the Amendment emanated from the states which felt that the Centre was intervening directly at the local level, and also attempting to introduce uniformity in the country. The way the prime minister went about consulting the district collectors considerably influenced the view of the states; they felt the effort was to bypass the states and reach the local level directly through centrally sponsored schemes. They also perceived it as an encroachment on their rights to legislate on panchayats. The amendment was again taken up by Narasimha Rao (who became prime minister after Rajiv Gandhi). Many of the concerns expressed during the earlier debate were taken care of, and it was enacted into a law in 1993. With this amendment—and another one for urban government—local governance got constitutional support.

These amendments made it mandatory for each state to constitute Local Self-Government Institutions (called Panchayati Raj Institutions, or Panchayats, for short, in rural areas) at the village, intermediate, and district levels (except for states with fewer than 20 lakh people). The amendment left the devolution of powers to the discretion of the state legislatures when it said that

> (It) may by law endow the Panchayats with such powers and authority as may be necessary to enable them to function as institutions of local self-government [with respect to] a. the preparation of plans of economic development and social justice; b. the implementation of schemes for economic development and social justice as may be entrusted to them, including those in relation to matters listed in the Eleventh Schedule. (For subjects listed in the Eleventh Schedule, see Appendix 1.)

In its provisions, the Act was not mandatory and allowed the states to respond at will. The scope of responsibilities, particularly those concerned with law and order, was excluded and subjects in the Eleventh Schedule were only suggested. The result of this design is that while the Constitution mandated a structure and suggested the extent of autonomy to be given, it was the states that decided how the structure was going to function, and the extent of autonomy to be given, by enacting their own legislations.

However, the Act made several significant advances over the past. It made it mandatory that elections will be held every five years, and will be conducted by State Election Commission. A uniform three-tier structure was envisaged, with the *gram sabha* (the village assembly) being the deliberative body of decentralized governance and the foundation of the panchayat system. Women's empowerment was mandated by reserving one-third seats in all the elected bodies as well as for the office of chairperson in each tier. Rotation of constituency was also mandated in these cases. Reservations for Scheduled Castes and Tribes were also provided. To ensure adequate financial resources to the panchayats, the Act has envisaged the setting up of a State Finance Commission every five years. District Planning Committees were made mandatory and given constitutional status.

The amendment marks a significant shift from past thinking about Panchayati Raj and is a move towards participatory democracy in making the gram sabha responsible for monitoring and evaluating local-level developmental programmes. It has also been given the responsibility of identifying the beneficiaries of a particular programme. The participatory character of the amendments can also be found in the effort to assure participation in the decision-making processes of those citizens who are usually excluded for social, economic, or gender reasons. Thus, women and Scheduled Castes get reservation in seats at assembly as well as functionary levels.

In addition, the provision of an Election Commission assures regular elections, and that of the Finance Commission a statutory provision of funds not dependent on the political leadership of the day. District Planning Committees have also been mandated. The cause of the decline of the panchayats in the earlier phase was laid at the door of infrequent elections and inadequate finances. This weakness has now been rectified.

A virtual democratic revolution has been brought about, with 30 lakh representatives getting elected at the local level every five years, out of whom 10 lakh are women and more than six-and-a-half lakh are dalits. Women and dalits are also occupying positions as heads of panchayats. Box 1 provides a glimpse of the emerging contours of the democratic revolution after the 1993 amendment.

Box 1 Democratic Base

District Panchayats:	532
Block/Tehsil/Mandal Panchayats:	5,919
Village Panchayats:	2,31,630
Total no. of elected seats:	30,00,000
No. of women elected:	10,00,000
No. of SCs/STs elected:	6,60,000

Note: Figures are approximate, adapted from Mathew (2000a).

As Chaudhri (2007: 169) points out, before 1994 the elected representatives closest to the voters were the members of the state legislative assembly. Now the panchayats—with each of its members representing a few hundred people—are closest to the voter. The Constitutional Amendments have been a major advance in supporting local democracy and decentralization. This can be sustained only if elections are held regularly and on schedule. What the amendment has done is to mandate the elections and not leave them to the vagaries of the state governments. The record has been fairly good until now—and more so as the state-level political parties are discovering the panchayat elections to be a good barometer of their own support in the rural areas. For, example, the fact that the Left was unlikely to win in its fight against the Trinamool Congress was judged from the fact that it lost support in the panchayat elections (*Asian Age*, 7 May 2011). In addition, the first entrants into panchayat elections also consider it their first entry into politics.

However, as we shall see in the following chapters—and notwithstanding this new-found interest in panchayat elections—this advance has not necessarily been matched by the states in delegating the necessary functions through their enabling legislations or administrative orders.

Panchayats as Self-Governing Institutions

Objectives of the Constitutional Amendment

The preamble to the 73rd Amendment to the Constitution begins by pointing out that even though the panchayats have been in existence for some time, they have failed to acquire 'the status and dignity of viable and responsive people's bodies'. Citing several reasons for this situation, the preamble goes on to lay down the goal of the amendment. It invokes Article 40 of the Constitution which enshrines one of the Directive Principles of State Policy: 'the State will take steps to organize village panchayats, and endow them with such powers and authority so as to enable them to function as *units of self-government'* (italics mine). The preamble states that the amendment was made to correct the shortcomings of the past, and to provide panchayat institutions with certainty, continuity, and strength. Among the shortcomings of the past, inadequate representation of SCs, STs, and women is specifically mentioned.

The 73rd Amendment set for itself the goals of creating panchayats as self-governing institutions, and increasing the participation of deprived groups in the decision-making processes of these institutions. The design of the initiative was that the Constitution will provide certain mandatory structures with a supporting system that would make these structures viable and capable of performing the functions given to them. The content of the functions and how they will be performed will be left to the states to legislate. Such a design took care of the objections from the states regarding the encroachment of the powers given to them by the federal character of the Constitution.

While meeting the concerns of the states, the design also played into the constraints of state-level politics. The actual performance of the amendment was dependent on the political will for decentralization in the states. Many critics have found this stipulation in the design a weakness in the initiative taken to establish panchayats as self-governing institutions, especially because while some states took up this task enthusiastically, others did not. Consequently, an all-India picture of the achievements and failings does not emerge.

Certain states—particularly West Bengal—stand out in terms of continuity, that is, from the time of the rejuvenation effort triggered by the Ashok Mehta Committee Report in 1978. Others—like Karnataka and Andhra Pradesh—joined in these efforts much before the amendment came into being, but lost out because of lack of political continuity. Kerala took up the decentralization project in mission mode, surpassing other states very enthusiastically after the passing of the amendment. However, West Bengal stands out because there was continuity in the political party that governed the state from 1978 to 2011. Interest in the panchayats was promoted because of the need to mobilize local support by political interests.

What becomes clear from the above is the vulnerability of the panchayat system and its dependency on the political interests of the party in power in a state. The design embedded in the 73rd Amendment has not been able to meet this challenge, and the performance of panchayat institutions continues to be dependent on state-level politics and its interests.

The amendment listed 29 subjects in the Eleventh Schedule for devolution to the panchayats. The number of subjects said to have been transferred varies from a few in number in some states to the entire list (see Appendix 1) as given in the schedule in some others. However, in all cases, progress in the delineation of functions of the different tiers of the local governments in matters concerning a given subject has been very slow. As the Second Administrative Reforms Commission says: 'Devolution has been sought to be done in most of the states by omnibus legislations regarding Panchayats/Municipalities and Municipal Corporations, in which the "matters" listed in the 11th and 12th Schedule are just repeated.'

Another dimension of the slow response of the conformity legislations to transfer subjects to the panchayats is the fact that the subjects given in the Eleventh Schedule are also given in the State list and the Concurrent list. The responsibility for administering programmes of poverty alleviation figures in both the lists. As a result, in some cases, even those activities that can be undertaken by local governments—

43

and have been devolved on them—are being undertaken by a number of government departments still functioning at the local level. These departments are being supplemented by the establishment of parallel bodies with functions that could be handled by the panchayats. Apart from many others, the Pradhan Mantri Gram Sadak Yojana is a good example of one such functional devolution.

A report of the Planning Commission (GoI 2001b) points out that

> [t]here are a plethora of Centrally Sponsored Schemes (CSSs) pertaining to 29 subjects being implemented by different Ministries and Departments of the Central Government. As per the Constitutional mandate in respect of 29 items of the Eleventh Schedule, three Fs, that is, functions, functionaries, and funds, have to be devolved on the PRIs for planning and implementation of schemes pertaining to a particular sector. In reality, the involvement of PRIs with respect to these 29 items has been minimal in most States. It has been observed that State Governments as well as Central Ministries have not taken concrete steps to integrate PRIs in their strategy of planning and implementation of CSSs under their purview.

The subjects that are sought to be transferred by the Constitution cover the broad spectrum of development activities. They include activities like education, health, child welfare, farm and non-farm activities, and infrastructure functions needed for socio-economic development. Most importantly, as Ghosh (2000: 58) points out, devolution is not restricted to development functions alone. The legislatures are free 'to endow the local councils with regulatory powers and authority as may be necessary to enable them to function as institutions of self-government'. This has not happened and, as seen above, the central and state governments have continued to occupy space that should have legitimately belonged to the panchayats. None of the states—with the probable exception of Kerala—have faced up to the challenge of creating self-governing institutions at the local level.

More recently, activity mapping is being undertaken by several states to ensure the effective decentralization of functions laid down in the Eleventh Schedule. This exercise is based on the subsidiary principle: any task that can be done at the local level should not be moved to a higher level.

45

Such a weakness notwithstanding, the amendment has provided for the devolution of development functions to an institutional framework at the local level which may be precursor to a three-tier federal system. This constitutionally mandated decentralization to democratic bodies may not be easy to erode. This has been the most important contribution of the constitutional mandate, and many have described it as the most revolutionary investment in the democratic development of the country.

The Institutional Structure and Elections

A three-tier institutional structure proposed in the amendment was accepted by all the states, and elections have been held every five years since the states passed their own legislations. There were a few exceptions, including Bihar. Panchayat elections were held in this state in 2001 even though the enabling panchayat legislation had been passed by the legislative assembly in 1993.

While a uniform structure has been laid down for all states, the amendment also stipulates that the intermediate panchayats may be dispensed with in states with a population of less than 20 lakhs. Otherwise, no size range for panchayats—either in terms of population or area—was laid down. The result is that the size of panchayats varies widely across the country, and this has its problems. There are several states like Punjab, Himachal Pradesh, and Maharashtra where gram panchayats have an average population of 2,000, while in Kerala and West Bengal, the averages are 23,598 and 17,218, respectively. There is similar variation in populations of intermediate levels in many states (see GoI 2006b).

The 73rd Constitutional Amendment envisages the *gram sabha* as the critical unit of the Panchayati Raj system. In its idyllic version, this is supposed to be the forum where villagers deliberate on their problems face-to-face, and give their demands to the gram panchayat, its executive body, for further action. The gram panchayat consists of 10–15 members, elected directly by the gram sabhas, which are construed as the agency not only of empowerment, but also of accountability. They were mandated to approve all plans and programmes of social and economic development, audit the panchayat accounts, and select beneficiaries for all types of programmes. It was hoped that this

47

provision would restrict the misuse of panchayats by the political leadership and the bureaucracy, and bring about a measure of transparency and accountability in the system.

While all states have provided for gram sabhas in their conformity legislations, little effort has been made to strengthen them with functional powers. In most states, therefore, gram sabhas are yet to take off. Kerala is an exception where there is recognition of their role, and where the panchayats need to explain the rationale of their decisions to the gram sabhas. They have also played an important part in local-level planning exercises. This has happened primarily because decentralization and the introduction of Panchayati Raj were adopted in the campaign mode, and sustained efforts were made to raise awareness on the issue. Gram sabha meetings were organized on holidays to identify local issues, and a large number of experts were mobilized to provide technical advice for local-level planning. Significant support came from a well-known non-governmental organization (NGO) in Kerala: the Sastra Sahitya Parishad.

In some other states, too, a few gram sabhas are generating a new atmosphere of participation and social audit. NGOs are playing innovative roles in capacity-building efforts. The Poorest Area Civil Society facilitated several village meetings in 2007–8 across Marathwada and Vidarbha to articulate the development-related demands of poor and marginalized families. The campaign covered 1,100 villages in 70 blocks of 11 districts in Maharashtra, and including three in Vidarbha. The effort was aimed at encouraging the poorer groups to participate in gram sabha meetings. There has also been support for strengthening the gram sabhas from NGOs like Mazdoor Kisan Shakti Sangathan (MKSS) in Rajasthan or Action Aid in Odisha. Several organizations provide training to a vast number of men and women elected to the gram panchayats in order to improve their understanding of the legitimate power they have acquired through an electoral process.

Despite all these efforts, however, gram panchayats have become more and more the instruments for implementing central schemes. They command little resources of their own. There are large schemes like the Mahatma Gandhi National Rural Employment Guarantee Scheme (MGNREGS) for infrastructure projects like irrigation, roads, water, repairs of community buildings, and so on. Funds are also available for welfare programmes like old-age pensions for widows and maternity pensions. In these schemes, gram panchayats serve to identify the targeted beneficiaries and monitor their performance. The gram panchayats also receive small grants to finance their local schemes. However, in most states, they do not have any direct control over the appointments of government-paid teachers or health workers.

Recognizing the need to strengthen the gram panchayats, in 2012 the minister of rural development announced that the Centre will spend Rs 900 crore on gram panchayats across the country beginning next year. This will help them implement local-level programmes. There is, however, silence on the issue of control over local functionaries, and making them accountable to the gram panchayats.

Elections

The Constitution now stipulates direct elections to the panchayats. With the appointment of State Election Commissions (SECs), there have been fairly regular elections to the panchayats in most states. However, in most cases, the SECs are dependent on the state governments for activities that lead up to the elections. In some states, they are not even empowered to issue notifications for the elections, a responsibility undertaken by the state governments themselves. Similarly, a number of state governments have retained the responsibility of the delimitation of constituencies and the preparation of electoral rolls. What this means is that delays in holding elections can be dependent on the timing of decisions of the state governments.

Another important dimension of the dependence of SECs on the state governments for the performance of their prime responsibility is in the area of reservations. The number of reserved seats in the panchayats is very high, and it is provided that there will be a rotation of constituencies for the purpose. In many cases, the state governments have delayed performing this function, and held up elections (see GoI 2007).

With no restrictions on political parties to mobilize support along their ideological persuasions, panchayat elections—now held regularly—have come to be seen as a significant method of measuring the strength of their local support base. Competitive politics has emerged as an important factor in elections in contrast to the earlier view of panchayats being conflict-free, and when prizes were given to panchayats that boasted of consensual decision-making. Gujarat has recently set a unique example. The State Government has announced incentives to the extent of Rs 1 lakh to those panchayats which would be able to hold elections on the basis of consensus. The scheme called *samras gram* (harmonious village) is clearly anti-democratic, and is regarded as a recipe for reward-induced guided democracy (Quoted in Datta 2009: 7). National-level political parties like the Congress and the Bharatiya Janata Party (BJP) compete for panchayat results. Recently, the BJP's victory in elections to the Goa assembly was sought to be buttressed by its victory in the panchayat elections as well, which was used to demonstrate state-wide support for the party (see Box 2).

With panchayat elections becoming barometers of local support, and panchayats receiving decentralized finances from state governments, elections are assuming other dimensions. Groups seemingly opposed to the state and rebelling against it have begun using the elections to garner public support for themselves and demonstrate the people's anger. In government circles, as Box 3 shows, 'it is ringing alarm bells'. However,

> Box 2   Parrikar Glad with Panchayat
> Election Results
>
> The BJP in Goa is thrilled with the panchayat elec-
> tion results. Posing for photographs with *gulal*-smeared
> victorious candidates, supported by the BJP in the
> panchayat elections, at the party head office in Panaji,
> Chief Minister Manohar Parrikar expressed happiness
> with the panchayat election results. Though it was still
> early in the evening, Parrikar said the indications and
> result trends showed that BJP had won in most areas of
> Goa 'with handsome margins'. Parrikar told TOI that
> in Sanquelim area, the BJP had 40 out of the 46 wards
> and in Shiroda, the BJP lost only about three wards.
> 'The position is very good,' Parrikar said.
>
> (*The Times of India*, 18 May 2012)

these developments are also serving the useful purpose
of co-opting recalcitrant groups into the legitimate fold
of democracy, and bringing them into the mainstream.

However, efforts at creating consensual, conflict-free
panchayats continue, and there have been reports of
the buying and selling of seats to create a semblance of
unanimity in several states (see Datta 2009).

In a quiet coup of sorts, Maoists have taken control of panchayats in about 30 blocks of Malkangiri and Koraput districts in the ongoing panchayat elections in Odisha. All their nominees have been elected unopposed after the Maoists warned local people against nominating any other candidate. Close to 2,500 members of these panchayats have also been elected unopposed. Sources said at least 32 heads of panchayats (*sarpanches*) have known Maoist links.

Wary that this could undermine anti-Naxal efforts by helping them expand their base, an alarmed Centre has asked the state government to step in. The main cause of worry is that panchayats have access to considerable funds under various social schemes including NREGS, besides what accrues from the devolution package.

A few months ago, Maoist groups had issued a call to boycott these elections in eight districts, including Malkangiri, Koraput, Kandhamal, Nuapada, and Nayagarh. This was followed by a more specific threat against candidates who attempted to file nominations without Maoist consent.

These districts benefit from the Backward Regions Grant Fund and much of it has to be implemented by panchayats. The prospect of Maoist groups controlling development funds and dispersing it as per their priorities, officials say, is a 'very disturbing trend'. The central government has asked security agencies to keep a close watch on the situation.

(*The Indian Express*, 16 February 2012)

Reservations

An important feature of the composition of the new panchayats—a major change from the ones that were established at the behest of Balwant Rai Mehta Committee Report—is the use of extensive reservations for women and the other deprived groups. Reservation for women was set at 33 per cent of seats at all levels of panchayats, including reservation for chairpersons. However, it was enjoined that there will be rotation of constituencies—a process that has been kept within the powers of the state governments in many cases. The representation of SCs and STs was stipulated to be according to the population residing in the area.

The reservation policy has led to the representation of 18.51 per cent SCs, 11.26 per cent STs, and 36.87 per cent women in all the 2,39,582 panchayats in the country. The number of elected panchayat members in the general category was 19,28,326 in 2008. In 2011, the central cabinet approved a proposal for enhancing reservation for women in panchayats from the present 33 per cent to 50 per cent. The provision will be applicable to all seats filled through direct election, office of chairpersons, and offices reserved for SCs/STs. An official amendment to the Constitution will be moved. This will raise the number of women representatives to around 14 lakh.

The impact of reservation on actual participation in decision-making is discussed in the next chapter.

Conclusion

The status of panchayats differs among states in the country. The experience of three states is relevant for this discussion. The enthusiasm with which the task of decentralization was undertaken has varied across states. Kerala took it up in mission mode, and its Campaign for Decentralized Planning carried out in 1996–7 stands out as the boldest and most comprehensive decentralization initiative yet to be undertaken in India. It has been contended that, from the very beginning, decentralization was a political project in Kerala, and thus the technocratic vision of incremental reform was rejected in favour of the 'big bang' approach. The State Planning Board allocated 35–40 per cent of plan expenditures to the panchayats in a single legislative Act. On the basis of a comparative study of Kerala, South Africa, and Brazil, (Heller 2001: 149) 'argues that to be successful, decentralization requires politically orchestrated action from above.' The ruling coalition led by the Communist Party of India (Marxist) (CPM) signalled a move away from state-bureaucracy development because it saw in decentralization a means of expanding its political base. Thus, Panchayati Raj was crafted as a political project.

The experience of Karnataka and West Bengal also seem to be amenable to this political explanation. In the mid-1980s, Karnataka initiated significant reform measures while West Bengal had taken the opportunity of the Ashok Mehta Committee Report to establish panchayats and make them instruments for implementing local development programmes. The CPM-led coalition ruling West Bengal for several years helped consolidate these decentralization efforts. The experiment in Karnataka lost its lustre once the Janata Party—which had a most enthusiastic Panchayat Minister Abdul Nazeer Sab—lost the elections.

Thus, while it is widely acknowledged that the amendments to the Constitution to set up institutions of local self-governance have been near revolutionary, there are several challenges in making them fulfil their promise. The first is a political one, signified by the reluctance of the state-level leadership in accepting the full implications of decentralization. Panchayats assure autonomy to the local people to govern themselves. There is a principle of subsidiarity wherein they are provided space to carry out activities that they can undertake at their level. Other activities can be the responsibility of the levels above. This principle has not been imbibed in actual practice. Devolution of powers listed in the Eleventh Schedule has been achieved more on a formal than substantive basis.

This follows from the weakness in the design stemming from the federal structure of the Constitution.

Most of areas listed in the Eleventh Schedule fall within the purview of the states, which are hesitant in empowering the local levels within them. In other words, the state-level leadership lends its strong voice while demanding more powers to the states from the Centre, but hesitates to grant the same when issues of empowering the local levels arise. The bureaucracy that has emerged from a tradition of centralized governance has also been wary of losing its hegemonic role. The result is that panchayats are seen as additions to—and not a replacement of—the administrative structure. A parallel administration headed by the collector continues to exist side by side with the panchayat. There seems to be a conceptual bind which continues to see the district collector as the centre piece of local governance.

The constitutional mandate, notwithstanding its weakness, has made panchayats an important arm of Indian democracy. This is evident in the interest shown by political parties in panchayat elections, including, paradoxically, even groups opposed to the state, as elections in Odisha or Kashmir have shown.

It does seem, however, that wherever NGOs have worked for the capacity-building of panchayats, they show better results. There is need to establish a more cooperative relationship between panchayats and civil society organizations to achieve better results in democratization at the local level.

Institutionalizing Panchayati Raj through constitutional means has to be enriched through a concomitant support system that brings about changes in the administrative system, and restructures Centre–State relations. Both the legal system and the administrative framework have to reflect the concerns of decentralization.

4

Devolution of Financial Resources to the Panchayats

As discussed earlier, panchayats have been established as self-governing institutions under the 73rd Constitutional Amendment. This was supposed to be a great advance from the previously existing panchayats that could not acquire this status for various reasons. While the amendment laid down the powers that needed to be provided to the panchayats in the Eleventh Schedule, state governments have acted merely in a formal fashion while doing so. This formality seems to pervade in matters of financial devolution also, as will be seen below.

An important dimension of decentralization is the ability of local institutions to raise financial resources to implement programmes within the powers allocated to them. There are limits to the amount of resources that can be raised locally. Hence, grants to these institutions become a significant part of their financial capacity to implement programmes. The Constitutional Amendment made these grants statutory, that is, not dependent on the whims of the central and state governments. This was a great change from the past, when the activities of the panchayats were tied to the funds allotted to them through the budgetary provisions of the Community Development Programme. As these funds dried up, panchayats also suffered from paucity of funds and gradually became dysfunctional.

Local Resources

The Second Administrative Reforms Commission has pointed out that, despite the important role that local bodies play in the democratic process and in meeting the basic requirements of the people, the financial resources generated by these bodies fall far short of their requirements. Figures indicate the abysmally low share of the revenues that the rural local bodies themselves generate in their total revenues. More than 93 per cent of their finances is derived from external sources.

A report of the Institute of Rural Management, Anand (IRMA 2008: 67) points out that in 15 major states, an average panchayat's own resources is less than 1 per cent of the state's own revenue. In an interesting calculation of a dependency ratio, the report shows how most states relied on external sources for their revenues. During the period 1998–9 to 2002–3, the ratio registered a decline in states like Karnataka, Andhra Pradesh, Haryana, Maharashtra, Rajasthan, Tamil Nadu, and Uttar Pradesh in comparison with the preceding five-year period. In interpreting the ratios, the report also underlines a caveat: less dependence may also mean that the state is not allowing enough to be done by the panchayats. It is no surprise, then, that they look more for external funds than making attempts to exploit their own resources (Ibid.: 71).

The panchayats' own revenues can come from tax and non-tax sources. In raising tax revenues, it must be emphasized that panchayats are too close to the people who are to be taxed. Potential revenues are related to agriculture, entertainment, levies on tractors and pumps, and so on. While these taxes are statutorily assigned to the panchayats, they can prove to be politically sensitive and difficult to administer. In general, the collections of a panchayat from its own revenues have been low. However, it must be mentioned that Kerala is an example in this regard. It was the highest performing state, collecting around Rs 43 per capita during 2002–3.

Another success story is based on research done in Tamil Nadu. Based on an analysis of three villages in Tamil Nadu, Sahasranaman (2012) argues that many gram panchayats today are in a position to substantially finance themselves, and build a culture of self-sufficiency, independence, and accountability to their citizens, reducing their dependence on devolutions from state governments.

State Finance Commissions

In order to provide stability and continuity to the functioning of panchayats, the Constitution has provided for State Finance Commissions (SFCs) under Article 143H. This provision lays down the procedure for the statutory transfer of funds from states to panchayats, thus replicating the functioning of Central Finance Commissions. It has made it obligatory for states to identify sources of tax and non-tax revenue, and make provisions for a share of funds from the Consolidated Fund of the state, and grants.

For this purpose, the governor of a state has been enjoined to appoint an SFC within a year after the conformity Act has been passed and, thereafter, every five years. The composition of the commission, the qualifications required for the appointment of its members, and the manner in which they are selected, is laid down by law. The SFCs have to make recommendations to the governor regarding the following matters:

1. the principles which should govern
   (i) the distribution between the state and the local bodies of the net proceeds of the taxes, duties, tolls, and fees leviable by the state, which may be divided between them under this Part, and the allocation between these bodies at all levels of their respective shares of such proceeds;
   (ii) the determination of the taxes, duties, tolls, and fees which may be assigned to, or appropriated by, the local bodies;
   (iii) the grants-in-aid to the local bodies from the Consolidated Fund of the state;

65

2. the measures needed to improve the financial position of the local bodies; and

3. any other matter referred to the Finance Commission by the Governor in the interest of sound finance of the these local bodies.

There appeared to be considerable enthusiasm in the states while appointing the first SFCs, and in implementing their recommendations. However, this enthusiasm has waned. A look at the information on the status of second SFCs provided by the Thirteenth Finance Commission shows that out of 15 major states, SFCs in two were yet to submit their reports. In eight states where reports had been submitted, the Action Taken Reports (ATRs) were not submitted to their respective legislatures. Only five states submitted their ATRs. In most of the states, the second SFC's period of coverage (that is, of recommendations) ended in 2005–6 (see Babu 2009).

States have been reluctant to devolve finance to the panchayats and make them as autonomous as possible. This reluctance emanates from various reasons. The approach adopted by the SFCs is not uniform. The Second Administrative Reforms Commission points out that while some states have followed the concept of pooling all revenues and then sharing them, others follow different percentages of devolution for different taxes. This reflects the diversity in laws regarding local bodies and in the functions assigned to them. In addition, the SFCs do not review state finances adequately in order to do their work of establishing a criterion, or the amount of transfers of state revenues. Unlike in the case of the Central Finance Commission, there is no tradition of state governments accepting the recommendations of SFCs. Thus, adequate resources are not committed to local bodies by state governments despite the SFCs' recommendations. One of the main reasons is that the state governments are not serious about appointing well-known experts to the commissions. More often than not, retired civil servants find a place in them.

In spite of all this, there are examples of states where not only were the recommendations accepted, but the funds, too, were quickly released. The IRMA report mentions that, in a rare case, rather than waiting for the next SFC, Haryana has gone ahead and released grants in advance.

One cannot conclude this section without noting that there are also some better performing states.

Among them are Kerala, Karnataka, and West Bengal. Kerala is the only state in which three SFCs have submitted their reports, and practically every recommendation has been accepted by the state government. The more important part of the state's financial devolution has been the provision of substantial funds for priorities set at the local level. This has been considerably helped by the People's Campaign for Decentralized Planning.

National Finance Commissions

The grants by the SFCs are sought to be supplemented by the grants recommended by the National Finance Commissions. The Tenth Finance Commission (1995–2000) was appointed just after the Constitutional Amendments had been passed in 1993–4. There was no mention of finances to Panchayati Raj Institutions (PRIs) in the terms of reference and, therefore, it recommended only *ad hoc* grants. The Eleventh Finance Commission also followed a similar practice because it noted that the tenures of SFCs were not congruent with the tenure of the Finance Commission—there was diversity in approaches, and there was delay on the part of state governments in finalizing the ATRs and placing them before the state legislatures. The Commission listed certain core sector services to support—drinking water supply, primary education, health, sanitation, and so on. It indicated that funds released should be earmarked for the operation and maintenance of these functions. The funds were untied otherwise, but could not be used for salaries and wages. Table 1 shows the amounts allocated by three Finance Commissions. Separate funds have also been earmarked for the maintenance of accounts and the creation of the data bases of the finances of local bodies.

TABLE 1   Amounts Allocated by Three Finance Commissions and Amounts Drawn by Local Bodies

Finance Commissions	Amount Allocated (Rs crore)	Percentage Drawn
FC X 1995–2000	4,380.93	66.46
FC XI 2000–5	8,000	82.52
FC XII 2005–9	18,000	92.58

Source: GoI 2009a: 151.

Over the years, there has been an improvement in the proportion of funds being drawn by the local bodies.

Centrally Sponsored Schemes

It is not as if the PRIs are not provided with adequate funds. The issue is that these institutions do not have adequate funds to pursue the functions that have been allotted to them; neither do they have enough funds to implement programmes at their discretion. They have increasingly become agencies to implement centrally sponsored schemes, leaving them with little freedom to pursue their own local concerns. These schemes include National Rural Employment Guarantee Scheme (NREGS), National Rural Health Mission (NRHM), Mid-day meals, Sarva Shiksha Abhiyan (SSA), Pradhan Mantri Gram Sadak Yojana (PMGSY), Accelerated Rural Water Supply Programme (ARWSP), Integrated Child Development Scheme (ICDS), Indira Awas Yojana (IAY), Rajiv Gandhi Gramin Vidyutikaran Yojana (RGGVY), and the Backward Regions Grant Fund (BRGF). The total amount of funds to be released directly to PRIs for 2009–10 is estimated to be Rs 95,000 crore. This poses quite a dilemma. While the institutions have substantial funds to implement centrally sponsored schemes, they do not have enough to implement programmes for their own local concerns. This converts the PRIs into implementing agencies of the central government rather than self-governing institutions.

It is pertinent to recall here that efforts to energize Panchayati Raj had been given up in the late 1960s because of the apparently successful experience of implementing schemes directly and through the administrative instruments of the central government. After the success in implementing the new agricultural strategy, policy planners began to believe that developmental schemes could be made successful if the central government continued to exercise control over them after initiating them, and if it monitored their performance to ensure conformity with pre-planned guidelines. During the Fifth Five Year Plan beginning in 1971–2, a spate of schemes was introduced by the central government to alleviate rural poverty. These were implemented at the local level, involved the state and district administration, but were planned and financed by the central government which kept a close watch to see that the implementation did not deviate from the pre-set guidelines. What evolved was an 'instrumental' view of Panchayati Raj. It was precisely to do away with this image of PRIs as agencies implementing government plans and programmes that the Constitutional Amendment of 1993 was passed, and hailed as a historic step towards the creation of self-governing institutions. However, it appears that the PRIs are now falling into a similar trap.

MPLAD Scheme

The Members of Parliament Local Area Development Scheme (MPLADS)—another policy decision taken recently—appears to be tightening the trap further. Just before the 73rd Amendment was passed, the then prime minister introduced a discretionary allocation of Rs 25 lakh per Member of Parliament (MP) per year to spend in his/her constituency for development projects reflecting the needs of the local people. This sum—to be utilized at the discretion of the MP—has grown over the years, and, during 2011, was increased to Rs 5 crore per year. The projects are implemented by the district administration, and the funds are directly sent to it once the project chosen by the MP is approved. It assumes the form of a centrally sponsored scheme. In most cases, the projects chosen are in the subject areas that have been devolved to the panchayats, but now bear the name of the MP, and thus come to be seen as part of his largesse. Interestingly, the guidelines issued by the Government of India for the implementation of this scheme states that 'A plaque for each work executed under MPLADS should carry the inscription "Member of Parliament Local Area Development Scheme work" indicating the cost involved, commencement, completion and inauguration, date, and the name of the MP sponsoring the project. The plaque should be permanently erected at the work place.'

For nursing his/her constituency, each MP has been provided with discretionary funds, thus depriving the PRIs of their legitimate due. Thus, there are around 800 MPs who would be spending Rs 5 crore per year—no meagre amount in total. In addition, many states have also given a similar discretionary fund to the Members of Legislative Assemblies (MLAs). However, the chief minister of Bihar has disbanded the local area development scheme for state legislators, thus rekindling the debate about whether or not elected representatives should perform the functions of the executive to implement development projects. The Left parties have opposed the MPLAD scheme on the same ground, saying that the job of MLAs and MPs is to deliberate on policy and frame laws. The Bihar MPs may not be able use the MPLAD scheme because the chief minister has also written to the Centre saying that the state government will not be able to implement the scheme unless the Centre creates a dedicated implementation machinery, or gives 6 per cent of the fund for implementing the scheme (*Hindustan Times*, 28 June 2011). Other critics have assailed the scheme as being anti-democratic and anti-decentralization. In a report, the Institute of Social Sciences (ISS), New Delhi, found the scheme to be against the very spirit of the Constitutional Amendment, which sought to empower local institutions. Demanding the abolition of the scheme, the ISS director George Mathew was forthright when he asked, 'What's the purpose of creating local bodies when parliamentarians will build toilets, streets, roads, and community buildings?' In his view, the scheme puts a question mark on the existence of the local bodies of governance.

District Planning Committees

Closely linked to the assurances given in the Constitution regarding the financial stability of the panchayats are the concerns about local-level—or grassroots—planning. Local-level planning has not been functional from the time it was first suggested in the First Five Year Plan in 1951–2. Since then, several efforts have been made. A District Development Council was established in the late 1950s to develop district plans and, subsequently, several government committees were formed to suggest ways to strengthen local planning methods and procedures. The Dantwala Committee on Block-level Planning was formed in 1978. The problem was examined again in 1984 through the Working Group on District Planning, headed by C.H. Hanumantha Rao. The Working Group recommended a greater decentralization of functions, powers, and resources in the interest of more meaningful district planning. It also recommended the setting up of district planning bodies of about 50 members, with the collector as the chief coordinator. This planning body was to be assisted by planning officers and technical experts at various levels. Other notable recommendations on strengthening planning and administration at the district level came from the G.V.K. Rao Committee on Administrative Reforms for Rural Development (1985), and the Sarkaria Commission for Centre–State Relations (1988).

However, these efforts at strengthening decentralized planning were not entirely successful. Some states like Kerala, Karnataka, and Maharashtra put in some semblance of local planning activity before the amendment was passed. To make decentralized planning mandatory, the Constitutional Amendment, through its Article 243ZD, created District Planning Committees (DPCs) to consolidate the plans prepared by the panchayats and municipalities in the district, and to prepare a draft development plan for the district as a whole. This committee would be an elected body, and the members would be elected from among the elected members of the panchayats and municipalities at the district level in proportion to the ratio between the rural and urban population of the district. The state legislature was given the power to decide the manner in which the chairperson of this committee would be appointed.

In spite of this mandatory provision, the proper functioning of DPCs has not been high on the agenda of state-level planners and administrators. In 2006, a government committee, under the chairpersonship of V. Ramchandra, came out with a report suggesting measures to revitalize local-level planning. In 2009, the

Society for Participatory Research in Asia (PRIA), an NGO, evaluated the work of the DPCs. Both reports expressed concern that decentralized planning is yet to become effective in the country. While most states carried out amendments of their respective state Acts to conform with the 73rd and 74th Amendments, the implementation of the provisions was not uniform in all cases. While the process of setting up elected bodies was carried out, and SFCs were formed to provide for financial devolution to these bodies, the formation of DPCs was neglected (see Appendix 3).

There is no doubt that, in most states, DPCs have been established. However, the composition of these committees in some states is not according to the Constitution, and most have not performed their functions as expected. The important feature of this committee is the integration of rural and urban local bodies in the framing of a district plan. It is quite probable that the creation of such a mechanism has been a stumbling block. Another reason is the lack of adequate discretionary funds available to these local bodies. For effective planning, the financial resources available need to be clearly identified.

Finally, it appears that the functions of each level of panchayats regarding the 29 subjects allocated in the Eleventh Schedule have not been demarcated. Under governmental direction, each level is now conducting what has come to be known as 'activity mapping'. The activity mapping now being undertaken by states is being done in the expectation that it will clearly identify the functions that are to be performed at each level of the panchayats. This will help in assessing the revenues required, and assigning its sources. In addition, it will help in the devolution of functionaries to implement these activities.

In conclusion, it is important to highlight one consequence of this lack of financial resources coupled with little planning: there does not seem to exist a clear vision of what the future development of local areas is going to be. A large number of schemes are individually implemented, but they are not integrated into a long-term plan. The object of district planning is to arrive at an integrated, participatory, and coordinated idea of the development of a local area. In the run-up to the Eleventh Plan, the Expert Group has recommended that the development of such a vision is a prerequisite for effective planning for a district.

In the absence of such a vision and a plan of action which can set the priorities, the districts do not become strong claimants for discretionary funds. They get embroiled in acting as agencies to implement centrally sponsored or MPLAD schemes. The failure to establish effective district planning agencies also indicates that while funds for a variety of central and state schemes are directed to rural administrative agencies, the elected bodies are yet to participate in the planning and implementation process. This further weakens the concept of self-governance that was the bedrock of the Constitutional Amendment.

5

Reservation for Disadvantaged Groups and their Participation in Decision-making

A signal contribution of the 73rd Constitutional Amendment has been the mandatory provision of reservation of seats for disadvantaged groups at all the levels of panchayats. It has been stipulated that there will be reservation of 33 per cent of seats for women, 15 per cent for the Scheduled Castes (SCs), and 7½ per cent for the Scheduled Tribes (STs). While the representation of SCs and STs was assured in the Constitution already, this amendment brought in the entirely new provision for women. This provision is historic, particularly if seen in the context of the failure to provide for women's reservation in the Parliament.

For the last 15 years—from the time of the prime ministership of Rajiv Gandhi—a Women's Reservation Bill was sought to be moved in Parliament. Several prime ministers have put their weight behind the bill, but it has failed to become law. It has been scuttled for one reason or the other. In 1996, it had a successful passage in the Rajya Sabha, but failed to muster support in the Lok Sabha. It is for this reason that women's reservation in panchayats has been a signal contribution of the 73rd Amendment to the Constitution.

Recommendations for strengthening the representation of women in panchayats have been made earlier, but they were not successful, being only recommendatory in nature. The Balwant Rai Mehta Committee Report had suggested that a 20-member *panchayat samiti* should co-opt or nominate two women interested in working for women and children. Maharashtra, Haryana, Punjab, and Rajasthan had followed this recommendation in their legislations, but the record had been poor, with very few getting elected. (One exception was the existence of an all-women panchayat in the Nimbut village of Pune district in Maharashtra in 1963–8.) Clearly, the provision of nomination or co-option was either an opportunity for patronage or mere tokenism. It was the mandatory provision of the 73rd Amendment that sought to undo this.

Gender Disparity and Development in India

Among disadvantaged groups, women appear to be more disadvantaged than other groups. The *Global Gender Gap Report 2007* (quoted in GoI 2008) ranks India 114 out of 128 countries, using a composite index of economic participation, educational attainment, political empowerment, health, and survival. It places India below its South Asian neighbours Sri Lanka and Bangladesh.

The sex ratio is considered a good indicator of gender discrimination. According to the Census of 2011, it was 940 females per 1,000 males. There has only been a slight improvement as compared to the 2001 Census when the ratio was 933 women per 1,000 males. The states show a wide disparity, from the highest in Kerala with 1,084 females per 1,000 males, to the lowest in Haryana with 877 per 1,000 males. The maternity mortality rate is also high with 212 deaths per 1,00,000 reported for 2007–9 by Census 2011. Not surprisingly, higher rates of maternal mortality are more character-istic of rural and backward caste women.

Gender inequalities are further reflected in women's literacy and education. The overall literacy rate in India is 74.04 per cent, and among males it is 82.14 per cent. In comparison, the women's literacy rate is much lower at 65.46 per cent. Again, there are disparities among states: Kerala has a literacy rate of over 92 per cent, with males and females showing similar percentages. In Andhra Pradesh, Bihar, and Uttar Pradesh, the lit-eracy rate falls between 64 and 69 per cent, with wide disparity in male and female literacy. The enrolment rate of girl children in schools is much lower than that of boys, and half the girls drop out before they reach middle school. In addition, women suffer from inequities stemming from a rigid and hierarchical caste system. Surveys have also been carried out to show that even women who earn have little say in household decisions. Differences in the status of women among the states seem to impact on the levels of their partici-pation in panchayats.

It is in this kind of social context that the manda-tory provision for reservations has been made. In most states, the proportion of women representatives hovers around 33 per cent. In Bihar, it is around 50 per cent for that is what the statute has made mandatory. Bihar's example was followed by Sikkim, which increased the reservation for women to 40 per cent, and held panchayat elections under the new arrangement in January 2008. Chhattisgarh, Madhya Pradesh, Rajasthan, and Uttarakhand have passed laws increasing the reservation for women in panchayats to 50 per cent. These changes will apply in the next panchayat elections in those states. In Karnataka, the proportion of women representatives is around 40 per cent, higher than the mandatory figure in that state.

Reservation has played a major role in widening the democratic base of women; indeed, around 80 per cent of all the women elected are from reserved seats. It has also motivated many women to contest elections and participate in the political process.

Structural Constraints

In the provision of reservation for women, one constraint has been introduced by the mandatory rotation of seats among constituencies from one election to the next. In most states, a woman cannot be re-elected from the same constituency, once her five-year term expires. This denies a woman the chance to nurse her constituency. Some states have introduced the two-child norm as an eligibility criterion for contesting elections. This makes it impossible for women with more than two children to stand for election. While this is applicable to both men and women, it is particularly detrimental for women since most of them do not have any control over reproductive decisions. Opinion against this provision is growing, and many of the states which had introduced it are revoking it.

Another deterrent to the participation of women is the abuse of no-confidence motions, a practice that is rampant to unseat women, dalits, and tribals elected on reserved seats. Some states, like Kerala and Himachal Pradesh, stipulate that only a woman will replace a woman if the post is reserved for women. In most states, such safeguards are not provided, giving rise to the assurance of tenure to political families, with women representatives who are surrogates of their husbands or other relatives who cannot stand for election due to reservation.

Participation in Decision-Making

Representation and participation are two different dimensions of democracy. It is relatively easy to legislate representation, but a far more complex and challenging task to create the conditions for participation. Proper representation does not automatically lead to proper participation. Moreover, not only institutional but social factors also influence participation. Institutionally, the way the quorum for meetings is devised has become an issue. Some states, like Chhattisgarh and Himachal Pradesh, have made special provisions in the quorum requirements in *gram sabha*s to ensure the presence of women.

Though many states have taken steps to assure the greater participation of women in the decision-making process, actual participation has not been easy. Participation also depends on the external environment in which panchayats function. In summarizing the characteristics of this environment, Palaniswamy (2010: 4) points to two key characteristics: first, the governance environment within which elected representatives work—measured by the sum of inequality, local power relations, gender differentials, caste-based divisions, and the different ways in which all these factors coalesce in different states—is critical to the effectiveness of the reservation policy; second, the extent of domination of institutions of local government by the local political and social elite. Thus, the governance environment lies at the heart of the question of the effectiveness of representatives on reserved seats, and of reservation policies.

As caste rigidities or patriarchal practices differ from state to state, participation by marginalized groups does not present a uniform picture across the country. In addition, over the years, the background characteristics of women and dalits have also changed. Both health and educations standards have changed, and differently across states.

However, there is anecdotal evidence to suggest that there are many elected women leaders who, fighting against odds, have attempted to address the more vital local needs. Usually, their focus has been on programmes related to women. Thus, they work on schemes for bringing piped water into the village; inspect development works, and nutrition centres under the Integrated Child Development Services (ICDS); and pay particular attention to children's education. They also take the initiative in a variety of family and matrimonial matters: from abusive or alcoholic husbands to settling land disputes (CWDS 1999: 137, quoted in Jayal 2003).

There are many cases of an individual *pradhan* or the *sarpanch* who has done commendable work despite heavy odds (see various issues of *Panchayati Raj Update*, from 1997 onwards). In West Bengal, Kamala Mahato, a panchayat pradhan in Purulia district, stands out as one who is commended for digging 10 wells for drinking water as well as for irrigation, and initiating employment schemes under the Integrated Rural Development Programme (IRDP). Similarly, the story of Fatimabee, a sarpanch in a village in Andhra Pradesh, caught the national imagination. She wore the traditional burqa and was illiterate, but managed to get many things done for her village. Again, women members of a gram panchayat in the Akola district of Maharashtra were fed up with the drinking habits of their husbands and the atrocities following the drinking sessions. They were successful in closing liquor shops that were doing brisk business in their village for the last 20 years.

In a more recent example, Tara Devi, elected as sarpanch of Samerdha Nosera village of a panchayat in the Bikaner district of Rajasthan in February 2010, is now a household name in the region, thanks to her dedication to the cause of protecting the girl child. As a result of Tara Devi's efforts, the child sex ratio has considerably improved in Samerdha Nosera, with a recent survey revealing 1,014 females against 984 males. Cases of maternal infant mortality have come to an end, and there is no case of girl child dropouts from schools. Situated 113 km away from Bikaner, Samerdha Nosera is among 20 village panchayats in the district included by the Sangam Matri Mission Sansthan in a project for 'Strengthening Gender Response of Panchayats in Rajasthan' initiated by PRIA (*The Times of India*, 5 January 2012).

However, such success stories are few and far between. Most others are overwhelmed with examples of exclusion and the way this is brought about. Social constraints include the following: (i) the patriarchal ordering of society that leads to tokenism and surrogate representation; (ii) illiteracy, which deprives women's participation in decision-making; and (iii) low-caste position combined with caste oppression and patriarchy. One of the most extreme forms of social constraint has been physical violence to which many women and lower-caste representatives have been

Box 4 Saas–Bahu Join to Script a Success Story

Most soap operas depict a fight between mother-in-law and daughter-in-law leading to considerable domestic tension. Movies are no different. When it comes to politics, women are remote-controlled by their husbands or their relatives. Like in many other parts of the country, the story in Rajasthan is no different where husbands take decisions on behalf of their wives. They are known as *sarpanchpati*s. But the story in Kasar village of Kota is different where two women smartly circumvented the law and brought name and fame to the panchayat.

Their interesting story has its genesis in the reservation of *sarpanch* for a dalit woman. Villagers found it difficult to zero in on a suitable person among the dalit communities and identified Himmat Bai, 32, who worked for a voluntary organization for the post. But there was a problem. She was ineligible for she had three children and the stipulated norm was that of two. The villagers were caught on the horns of a dilemma and were wracking their brains when they were baffled by a proposal from her mother-in-law, Para Bai. She proposed that the villagers could elect her as sarpanch and, together with her daughter-in-law, she would serve the community. Para Bai fulfilled the requirement of the two-child norm. Villagers knew that they were circumventing the law, but they trusted her and voted for her.

As a result, Para Bai won the elections with a clear majority and brought her daughter-in-law to the office along with her. During the last two years, both the women have been working hard to develop infrastructure in the village, and for community welfare. PRIA, the NGO supporting the women, points out that the panchayat consists of a population of about 7,600, has a congenial atmosphere for women, and reports of violence against them or those of female foeticide are not reported.

(Based on a report by P.J. Joychen, *Deccan Herald*, 20 May 2012)

subjected. This coercive mechanism of exclusion is more serious than simple disfranchisement that comes from illiteracy or patriarchal values that are enforced or internalized (Jayal 2003: 42). There is increasing concern about violence perpetrated on elected women representatives.

BOX 5   Panchayat Bans Girls from
Seeking Share

A village panchayat in Haryana has banned daughters
from seeking share from the parental property in Thua
village of Jind district. The village panchayat was held
on 4 May 2012 and the resolution was passed under
the signature of a woman *sarpanch*, Rani. More than
400 persons attended the meeting. The panchayat made
it clear that the married girls won't be allowed to sell
their piece of land. The spokesman Amar Lal Kaliramna,
known as *pradhan* in the village, further added that
the entire village would oppose anybody who tries to
purchase such land.

(Adapted from a report in *The Times of India*,
12 May 2012)

Recently, in a meeting organized by the All India
Dalit Mahila Adhikar Manch, elected dalit women representatives from Bihar, Uttar Pradesh, and Rajasthan
highlighted stories of discrimination and violence perpetrated against them. Most of them complained that
the police and administration did not support them.
Syeda Hameed, member of the Planning Commission,

said the status of dalit women representatives was the same as it was years ago (see *The Hindu*, 8 February 2012).

Thus, despite reservation, women's participation is still a struggle. Legislative Acts have given women avenues of empowerment, but social constraints appear as serious obstacles. In Tamil Nadu, the Tamil Nadu Federation of Women Presidents of Panchayat Government and the Tamil Nadu Federation of Dalit Presidents of Panchayat Government have been fighting for their rights. In the past few years, many more networks of elected women representatives have been created; the most notable experiments in networking and association formation have taken place in Karnataka, Gujarat, and Kerala.

Representation of SCs (Dalits)

The caste system in India has systematically discriminated against dalits and prevented their participation in the social, economic, and political life of mainstream society. In this peculiar system of social stratification, the bottom categories of people in the social hierarchy have been treated as untouchables and outcastes. This

has forced them to live a life of destitution and deprivation. Historically, these groups have been subjected
to economic and social exploitation. The system bars
mobility by creating hierarchical occupational categories, and thus has forced these groups to continue
to do work that involves demeaning tasks. The social
distance between this category and the upper castes is
defined by rituals sanctified by custom and religion.

Traditionally, village affairs were controlled by the
upper castes, with dalits being separated geographically
in hutments far away from upper-caste houses. The
exploitative situation was aggravated in rural areas, and
it was this that Dr Ambedkar called attention to in the
Constituent Assembly when he damned the village as
nothing 'but a sink of localism, den of ignorance and
narrow-mindedness'. Around 75 per cent or more of
dalits are landless, or near landless. This reduces most
dalits in rural areas to being agricultural labourers, and
their literacy rate is much lower than the rest of the
population. While the Indian Constitution has sought
to ameliorate their social and economic condition
by providing for legal safeguards against caste-based
discrimination, the effective participation of dalits in
local village affairs remains a very formidable problem

because discrimination against them is embedded in social history.

Under Article 243D, the Constitutional Amendment has mandated that seats will be reserved for SCs at all levels of panchayats in proportion to the number of dalits in the area. Out of these, one-third will be reserved for women. It has left it to the state legislatures to determine the reservation of chairpersons at the panchayat or other levels. According to prevalent law, the reservation of seats mandated by the Constitution has been 15 per cent in educational institutions and others.

The population of dalits varies across the states. The highest proportion of dalits to the total population is in Punjab. But dalits are primarily concentrated in Uttar Pradesh, West Bengal, Tamil Nadu, Andhra Pradesh, and Bihar. These states account for 53.6 per cent of the dalit population in the country. The proportion of dalits also varies across districts. However, in general, the states have adopted the constitutional proportion of 15 per cent for reservation rather than the proportion of dalits residing in any panchayat area. This has meant that whether they are less or more, the same proportion applies. This has created problems of participation in actual practice.

However, even after they have secured representation, dalits face severe challenges. Santha (2002: 1953) recounts events in four gram panchayats in two districts of Tamil Nadu where dalits were denied the democratic right to contest elections even for the reserved seats. Finally, elections were held in 2006 in defiance of the local people. According to the Institute of Rural Management, Anand (IRMA) report, this gave hope to the dalit presidents who believed it was the first step towards empowering dalits in some parts of the state. However, within a month, the dalit president of another panchayat was murdered. In contrast, in Bihar, following a Patna High Court order—against which an appeal has been pending in the Supreme Court since 1996—as many as 124 dalit candidates have registered their presence as *mukhia*s (*Panchayati Raj Update*, October 2002: 1952).

Participation of Dalits in Decision-making

Providing reservation for disadvantaged communities is one set of institutional mechanisms that seek to empower the dalits. However, it is not a sufficient condition for their participation in the decision-making process. The barriers to the participation of dalits in decision-making are embedded in historical practices of social exclusion. Their entry into institutions where the upper castes have ruled has come as a threat to entrenched groups. Various methods, like the ones used to silence women representatives, have been applied here too.

However, the experiences vary widely. In an empirical study conducted by Narayana (2005), the findings are revealing. The study was conducted in one block each of Madhya Pradesh, Tamil Nadu, and Kerala. The participation of dalits was as good as that of others in the gram sabhas. The most significant finding was that the participation of the poor in Kerala is higher than in the other two states. These findings are corroborated in many ways in different states. In their study on West Bengal, Ghatak and Ghatak (2002) mention that the average attendance in *gram sansad* was low at 12 per cent (10 per cent is the quorum), but they highlight the fact that, generally, the participation level is low for all categories, and so also of those of the disadvantaged category. Similar findings emerge also from studies conducted in Madhya Pradesh (Beher 2001) and Karnataka (Deshpande and Murthy 2002).

Dalits suffer from discrimination and oppression that arise not only from social reasons, but also from the way in which upper castes formulate rules and regulations. In Gujarat, the Panchayati Raj Act stipulates a social justice committee in every village, and makes it responsible for the disposal of animal carcass. This is a clear case of the practice of untouchability which goes unchallenged. A dalit voluntary group—the Gujarat Rajya Gram Panchayat Samajik Nyaya Samiti Manch—has planned to go to court on this, but political leaders have remained silent on its effort to mobilize support (*The Indian Express*, Ahmedabad, 9 February 2009). Severe punishments are meted out to whole communities of dalits by upper castes in cases of boy–girl relationships. In most states, the social justice committees do not function.

Evidence from most states show that the relations among the panchayat members are caste-based and unequal. Dalits suffer severely on this count; however, the relations are better wherever the sarpanch also belongs to the reserved category. Based on her research study, Palaniswamy (2010) argues that

[A]lthough the relevance of caste is not surprising, the answer to the question of how caste might matter is striking. In particular, the effectiveness of SC representatives depends on the caste identity of the gram panchayat president. SC representatives perform better when they interact with a reserved president—a result that suggests that shared identities, and therefore caste-based social networks, shape the effectiveness of reservation policy.

A number of explanations have been offered for the weak participation of dalits in an institutional environment where caste identity is an important feature of relationships. Mathew (2003: 48) has argued that this is mainly because of the lack of awareness, and the feeling among the disadvantaged groups that their views are not taken seriously, and their voices are not heard if the leadership is from dominant castes. Deshpande and Murthy (2002) have also argued that the long-term solution lies in increasing the levels of awareness while Beher (2001) suggests that participation is higher in areas where there is greater activity of the non-governmental organizations (NGOs). This echoes our earlier discussion on how the support of civil society organizations to disadvantaged groups empowers them, and builds confidence in them.

A more popular and widely held explanation is that these problems are embedded in the wider socio-economic and political context in which the dalits are placed. The issue of participation is related to the radical transformation of society and the socio-economic upliftment of these groups. The Ashok Mehta Committee Report (GoI 1978a: 91) had argued that developments likely to take place in the socio-economic structure of the country during the next decade will determine the future role of the Panchayati Raj Institutions (PRIs), especially with reference to the weaker sections. At the local level, the particular reference has been to the inability to undertake land reforms to weaken the hold of the dominant castes. There is no doubt that structures of social and economic oppression have to be dismantled before the dalits can benefit from the opportunities provided by reservations and the access to local institutions.

In assessing the participation of women and dalits in panchayats, some anecdotal evidence of individual cases of dynamism and success exist. On the other hand, there are also stories of women who have been physically abused by male members wanting to have their way. Dalits have also suffered in a similar way. Much of the resentment against these groups is embedded in the social system and the prevalence of caste discrimination. The rise of women in public life goes against the tenets of a rigid patriarchal system, and the acceptance of dalits as equal partners in decision-making goes against the rigidities of the hierarchical caste system. It must be underlined that women and dalits appear to be at the bottom of both hierarchies and suffer the consequences of discrimination the most.

Tribals (Adivasis) and Panchayats

India's tribal people are spread throughout the country, except for Punjab and Haryana, and account for 8.2 per cent of the country's population. This spread of the population is dense in some areas like in the North-East, where around 90 per cent of the population is tribal, while in other states like Odisha, Madhya Pradesh, and Andhra Pradesh, it ranges from 20 to 30 per cent. The North-East areas were considered very backward, and were declared Sixth Schedule areas (covering Assam, Meghalaya, Tripura, and Mizoram in the North-East), while the Fifth Schedule covered the tribal areas of the rest of the country. Currently, the

Fifth Schedule covers tribal areas in nine states, namely, Andhra Pradesh, Odisha, Jharkhand, Chhattisgarh, Madhya Pradesh, Maharashtra, Gujarat, Rajasthan, and Himachal Pradesh.

Such categorization into Fifth Schedule and Sixth Schedule areas is a legacy of the colonial administration which was incorporated into the Indian Constitution after independence. The purpose behind accepting such categorizations was the concern for protecting the economic life of the tribals, and for safeguarding their customs and institutions.

Panchayat Extension to Scheduled Areas (PESA) Act

A special effort was made to provide tribals the opportunity to exercise their right to self-governance through the enactment in 1996 of a special law known as the Panchayat Extension to Scheduled Areas (PESA). When the 73rd Constitutional Amendment was brought into effect, many states (like Madhya Pradesh and Andhra Pradesh) extended it to areas which had substantial tribal populations. These were the areas covered under the Fifth Schedule. A public interest litigation was filed in the Supreme Court, raising issues regarding the special features of natural resource management in these areas. The Supreme Court intervened, and directed Parliament to take specific measures for local governance in the scheduled areas.

In response to the directive of the Supreme Court, the Parliament appointed a committee under the chairmanship of a tribal MP from Madhya Pradesh, Duleep Singh Bhuria, to make recommendations for special provisions. Based on the Bhuria Committee Report, the PESA Act 1996 was passed by Parliament. The Act extends to the tribal areas of nine states, namely, Andhra Pradesh, Chhattisgarh, Gujarat, Himachal Pradesh, Jharkhand, Maharashtra, Madhya Pradesh, Odisha, and Rajasthan. Under the Act, gram sabhas are endowed specifically with such powers and authority as to enable them to function as institutions of self-government. These powers are related to the following:

1. Ownership of Minor Forest Produce
2. Enforcement of prohibition
3. Prevention of alienation of land

4. Control of local plans and resources, including the Tribal Sub-Plan
5. Management of village markets
6. Control over moneylending to STs.

In a way, this legislation was of great significance. It recognized the right of tribals over the natural resources on which their livelihood depends, and also their autonomy in sustaining their own culture. It was for this reason that PESA attempted to vest legislative powers in the gram sabha.

The PESA Act was meant to enable tribal society to assume control over its own destiny, and to preserve and conserve its traditional rights over natural resources. The law affirms that the customs, traditions, and religious practices of tribal people be restored and preserved. It also affirms their cultural identity and right over natural resources. Any legislation on the panchayats for the tribal areas is to be in consonance with the customary laws, social and religious practices, and traditional practices. The Land Acquisition Act, which enables the State to take over any land for 'a public purpose', is based on the principle of individual ownership, and does not take cognizance of the customary regulation of common property resources in tribal areas. As Kothari (2007: 289) points out, among many tribal communities, land and such other natural resources are owned jointly by the community, and their use by individuals is sanctioned by it.

In reality, however, the passage of the PESA Act has not led to the kind of tribal empowerment that it envisaged. There appear to be many reasons for this; however, primarily, the issue of tribal autonomy to control local resources has not entered the mainstream political and policy discourse. Central and state laws relating to mining, forest produce, water resources, and more importantly, the Land Acquisition Act are not convergent with the provisions of this Act. A study conducted in Odisha found a considerable gap between the principle and the practice of self-governance in the tribal panchayats (Ratho 2007). Table 2 presents some of the contradictions that have emerged.

Most of the tribal areas fall in heavily forested regions, and have minerals which are much in demand. There is continuous pressure on these areas from powerful industrial interests for forest products and the extraction of resources from mines. In its pursuit of economic growth, the Indian state has joined this

TABLE 2 Principle and Practice

Principle	Practice
Every gram sabha is competent to preserve and safeguard its community.	MoUs for mining and industrialization are signed between the government and multinational corporations without consultation with affected tribal people.
Gram sabha or panchayat at the appropriate level should be consulted before the acquisition of land in Scheduled Areas for development projects.	Consultations with gram sabha for land acquisition are organized by the district administration in the presence of an armed police force.
Gram sabha in tribal areas is endowed specifically with powers to enforce prohibition, or to regulate or restrict the sale and consumption of any intoxicant.	The state government of Odisha decided to open 2,000 liquor shops in different districts.

effort. New industries dependent on the resources available in these areas are coming up and depleting the sources of livelihood of the tribals living there, resulting in struggle, conflict, and violence.

In the last decade, water resources have also come under the purview of the demands of multinational soft drink industrial companies. In March 2000, the Perumatty gram panchayat in Palakkad district of

Kerala granted a licence to Coca Cola to set up its bottling plant in the village Plachimada on a total area of 35 acres. Coca Cola began extracting 5,00,000 litres of groundwater from six bore wells and two dug wells. Of this, while 1,50,000 litres was used in the manufacture of the beverage, the remaining was used in incidental activities like the washing of the bottles and the treatment of the effluent generated as a result of subjecting the extracted water to a process of reverse osmosis for ensuring the purity of the water mixed with the concentrate. Within two years, there were numerous complaints from the communities residing around the plant of acute drinking water scarcity and environmental problems. As a result, the panchayat cancelled the licence on 15 May 2003, after considering Coca Cola's reply to the notice issued to it by the panchayat. Upon a challenge to this decision by Coca Cola, the state government put the cancellation on hold, and directed the panchayat to constitute an expert committee to examine the soil and groundwater samples to ascertain the truth of the complaints.

Aggrieved by this decision, the panchayat petitioned the High Court of Kerala. A single judge accepted the contention that water was a public wealth, and its excessive extraction by a private actor could not be permitted by the state which was a public trustee of the precious community resource. Coca Cola was restrained from extracting further groundwater through the wells on its land. On appeal by the company, a bench of two judges of the High Court reversed the verdict of the single judge and directed the panchayat to renew the licence. This it did after receiving the report of an expert committee constituted by it, but it placed a number of restrictions. The plant has been lying idle since 2004. The case is now pending with the Supreme Court, with several appeals from Coca Cola, the panchayat, and the state government.

As a consequence of this discrepancy between what is provided for the gram sabhas in the Constitution and the lack of capacity of the government to enforce these provisions, resentment is rising in large areas where tribal land is being acquired for industrialization and mining. Large projects in predominantly tribal areas (Fifth Schedule areas) must follow the process of public consultation, which involves a public hearing (in which the assessment of the environmental impact of the project is presented) and a meeting of the gram sabha (where villagers and government officials agree on the terms and conditions of land acquisition). It is important to point out that although the Bhuria Committee, whose report forms the basis of the PESA Act, had recommended that the consent of the village community should be obligatory, the Act provides for consultation and not consent. While environmental public hearings do not mandate a quorum for project-affected persons, land acquisition rules formulated under PESA mandate that at least a third of the villagers must be present at a gram sabha—and a third of them must be women—when land is acquired in a tribal village to ensure that the proceedings are not hijacked by a small coterie.

A recent report summarized in Box 6 points out that officials in Chhattisgarh treat this process as a mere formality, and the provisions of PESA 1996 are given a go-by. They routinely overrule gram sabhas to acquire land on behalf of industries, prompting a withdrawal of the 'public' from public hearings. The report further quotes the Planning Commission and the rural development minister, both identifying the non-implementation of PESA as a factor in increasing tribal disaffection and the rise of violence in these areas.

Box 6   Of Mines, Minerals, and Tribal Rights

In Korba, the villagers were protesting the planned expansion of a 1,320 MW power plant set up by Lanco Amarkantak. 'Earlier, we gave our land willingly on the condition that company will give us jobs,' said Laharam Murao. He said that the company had acquired 1.5 acres of his land in 2005, but he had neither received any compensation nor anyone in his family gained permanent employment in the plant. This time there will be no public hearing and no land will be given. On 7 January, villagers from the affected villages blocked the road to the public hearing. The district collector arrived at about 3 p.m. and set up a table about 50 meters away from the people and announced that the public hearing had begun. After a few persons allied to the administration had spoken, the collector announced that the hearing was complete and tried to leave. It is at this point that the crowd grew restive and had to be controlled by the police.

In 2010, the Korba district administration scheduled land acquisition meetings in four villages—none of which met quorum requirements. A similar procedure was repeated in the villages of Khordal, Pehnda, and Saragbonda where gram sabhas were repeatedly rescheduled to work around the quorum requirements.

In an interview, the District Collector insisted that his office complied with all legal provisions governing land acquisitions. 'For all public hearings there is a protest ... but we go by the Act.'

(Summary from a report by Aman Sethi in *The Hindu*, 15 January 2012)

The rural development minister reiterated this view again while addressing a meeting of the newly elected members of PRIs in Maoist-affected areas in Odisha, saying that no tribal land would be acquired for any purpose without the consent of the *palli sabha*. Measures must be taken to ensure that adivasis (tribals) get the benefits of any mining done in their areas (*The Hindu*, 29 May 2012).

Access to and control over natural resources continues to be the most substantive matter in all issues concerning tribal people. There appears to be recognition at the highest levels of decision-making that the PESA—promulgated with the great ambition of providing space to the adivasis to have a say in governing their own affairs—has been ineffective. A committee of secretaries has been formed to look into improved implementation of PESA (see Box 7). In addition, concerned that the Forest Rights Act has yet to bring benefits to the majority of forest dwellers in the country, the Centre has told the state governments to expedite the implementation of the landmark 2006 legislation that seeks to transfer the ownership rights of forest lands to the people who have been living on them. In his letter, the tribal affairs minister has mentioned that the 'slow and tardy implementation of the Act went *against our professed adherence to law*' (italics mine for emphasis) (*The Indian Express*, 29 May 2012).

However, the government is faced with a dilemma: it leans against the tribals in its economic policy, but publicly professes support to the tribals in its political affirmations. Rapid industrialization entails the exploitation of natural resources—minerals, forest produce, water, and so on—which, in turn, leads to the displacement of people. Precedence has been given to the already existing laws of the state governments, and the spirit of PESA has not been adhered to. Major conflicts have arisen in cases of land acquisition, rights to forest produce, and mining rights, and the states have overridden the panchayats. Several large projects are

Box 7   Committee of Secretaries

A Committee of Secretaries (CoS) headed by Home Secretary G.K. Pillai has been formed to push for the speedy implementation of the Panchayat Extension to Scheduled Areas Act. The Act, implemented in 1996, intended to hand over greater powers to tribal communities over the land and resources, has remained a paper tiger though it was meant to provide entitlements instead of doles to the tribals. In pursuance of the two-track approach in the naxal-affected areas, the COS is now looking at synchronizing other laws and programmes of the government in the Schedule V areas, including the forest regulations and the Forest Rights Act.

As part of this move, the COS has tasked the Panchayati Raj ministry to look at how to bring benefits of the purported Rs 50,000 crore annual trade of minor forest produce to the communities. The ministry will be looking into the possibilities of turning the existing grey markets of hundreds of roots, tubers, leaves that are traded at extremely low margins by the forest-dependent communities into formal organized markets where the communities can get a greater percentage of the profits made from the lucrative trade.

(*The Times of India*, 23 July 2010)

under dispute, and are being stalled today with increasing resistance from tribals whose livelihoods are being wiped out. Many believe it is this alienation of the local tribal population that has created what has come to be known as the Naxalite movement.

6

Panchayats and the Web of Local Governance Institutions

Multiple systems of governance continue to exist at the local level even after constitutionally mandated self-governing panchayat institutions were introduced in 1993. Some of these are traditional institutions that have existed from colonial times, while others have been added to implement Central and state government policies as their development plans have unfolded since independence. Still others have emerged out of the new rhetoric of governance and neo-liberalism. In this network, panchayats are being perceived as one of the local-level governance institutions—and not as the primary one or as a third tier of the federal structure.

District Administrative System

Traditionally, district administration, with the collector as its head, is central to what happens at the local level in the rural areas. This institution is so well-entrenched that the new organizations like panchayats or non-governmental organizations (NGOs) are still struggling to find space in the area of local policymaking and implementation. As a matter of fact, such is the prominence of the collector in the Indian administration that no discussion of local-level issues can take place without bringing that position in the picture. This is because district administration was the most important instrument of colonial rule. However, despite this ancestry, very little change has come in its structure, and often in its role or behaviour, in the period after independence.

During the colonial regime, the district administration was rigorously built up to bring the totality of government closer to the people. It was a hierarchical sub-system of the state administration, performing specific tasks assigned to it. So long as revenue and law and order were the dominant considerations, the district collector was accepted as the pre-eminent officer at the district level. For the people, he was the government; around him revolved the entire administration of the area. From the British point of view, 'the maintenance of the position of the District Officer was absolutely essential to the maintenance of British rule in India, and any diminution in his influence and authority will be dearly purchased even by an improvement in the administration of justice' (Minutes of Sir Fitzaines Stephens writing in 1872, quoted in Potter 1964: 4).

So long as the tasks remained unchanged and local self-governing institutions were unborn or powerless, the system did not have to face competing forces. The real problems of the district administration started with the changes in its ecology.

After independence, development and planning became the key themes of policy discourse, and attention was diverted to nation-building activities. Revenue and law and order were not more important than road building, canal construction, educational expansion, agricultural development, and so on. While they were seen as the reflection of the urges of the people themselves, many of these activities required a high degree of technical know-how that was beyond the direct experience and training of the district collector. In many cases, the expertise in technical fields had to be provided from state-level departments who were to have more say in such matters than the district collector. The result was that the technical departments of the state government began to locate their officers at the local level to implement their programmes and projects. As these offices multiplied, the district administration became a more complex system than what it was under the colonial administration. The First Administrative Reforms Commission of 1969 tackled this problem of increasing complexity by concluding that 'as a result of our survey, we have generally come to the conclusion that there is nothing intrinsically wrong with the district administrative system. The system has stood the test of time, and even though it was basically designed to meet the colonial needs of the British, it can continue to serve the needs of a welfare state also.'

Thus, the district collector continued to enjoy the pivotal position in the local administration and, during the development era, became the chief coordinator of all programmes being implemented at the district level and below. In addition to his main duties of revenue collection and law and order, he is allotted any assignment that does not relate to any particular department, or of any department without a field office of its own for the district. He is the ex-officio district election officer and, after the introduction of the Community Development Programme in 1952, was designated as the district development officer.

The fact that the collector is the arbiter (as district magistrate) of local conflicts, land disputes, and law and order, gives him enormous powers at the local level. This leads to his primacy, a position which the administrators are loath to lose. In addition, the district collector is the eyes and ears of the Central and state government at the local level, a role that continues to be reinforced. Under the new dispensation in the conformity Acts, all state governments have provided necessary legislative provisions in their Panchayati Raj Acts to empower the district collectors to oversee malpractices and the misuse of powers by the panchayats. These range from the suspension of the panchayats to the suspension of the elected chairpersons. To take action in these matters, most state governments rely on the reports of the district collector who is usually named as the enquiry officer. This further enhances the status and prestige of the officer who represents the state government at the local level.

Panchayats are located in this kind of local administrative system which has traditionally been an instrument of control and regulation, and has subsequently also acquired developmental functions in the planning era. The 73rd Constitutional Amendment did not in any way transgress into the authority and responsibility of this system, which has grown to be quite complex over the years. An example of this is also the persistence of the District Rural Development Agency, headed by the district collector, established to implement the Integrated Rural Development Programme. Kerala and Karnataka are the only two states that have merged it with district panchayats. This has meant that poverty alleviation programmes continue to be implemented by this agency rather than handed over to the panchayats.

In addition, the two functionaries of the panchayats—the secretary and the executive officers—are not under the control of the panchayats, but are part of the state government bureaucracy. Moreover, most states have not transferred functionaries related to the 29 subjects devolved to the panchayats under the Eleventh Schedule, and the panchayats, therefore, have to work through the functionaries still within the state hierarchy. Kerala is the only state which has completely transferred the control of functionaries to its panchayats. More than 100 officials of different line departments have been devolved to district panchayats which exercise supervisory and administrative control over these functionaries.

The general picture that is emerging is that the panchayats have no or little control over the functionaries who have the responsibility of implementing schemes formulated by the panchayats within the subjects allotted to them. They also function within the framework of a powerful administrative structure that commands primacy at the district level as well as the confidence of the state governments. In other words, the panchayats still do not have any administrative autonomy.

Parallel Bodies

Limitations on the autonomy of the panchayats are exacerbated by the introduction of parallel bodies which implement schemes that squarely fall within the subjects allocated to the panchayats in the Eleventh Schedule, but which are independent of the panchayats in actual practice. These developments have taken place as India has opened up to multinational donor agencies whose major concern has been developing institutions that are efficient and economical in the delivery of services. The concerns of economy and efficiency are combined with the recognition that governments have failed to do the same with their bureaucratic and hierarchical framework. Alternative institutions had to be found.

Within the new governance discourse, great faith was placed on NGOs as engines of development. Donor agencies began to direct funds and resources directly to them, without governmental mediation. This led to the strengthening of NGOs, and more support in creating them where they did not exist at the local level. Most of these NGOs were linked to registered societies at the state level and enjoyed a great deal of freedom from bureaucratic and legislative control. They are not linked to panchayats and are not accountable to them. Most of them work in the areas of water supply, sanitation, health, and primary education. Thus, much of the developmental activity is taking place outside the panchayat system. Thus, as Chandrashekhar (2011) points out, while NGOs are flush with funds, panchayats do not have the wherewithal to perform even the minimum maintenance functions to improve the assets and utilities of the village.

Most of these NGOs have taken the shape of user committees, with the aim of providing participation to the beneficiaries of a particular service. These committees function in the areas of minor irrigation, education, forest management, and so on. International agencies view user committees as mechanisms to give local peoples a greater say in the development decisions that affect them. Their view of decentralization locates it in the dispersal of power, and reliance on civil society organizations—termed as stakeholders—in a particular activity.

It has been argued that the Swajal water project in Uttar Pradesh has demonstrated that community-driven development for rural infrastructure can be cost-effective and sustainable (Singh 2007: 186–219). The management of the project was located outside the government and water board. The Project Management Unit (PMU) was an autonomous registered society. The PMU and the local village communities—in the form of village and sanitation committees—took the help of NGOs for both hardware and software support. The members of these committees were the stakeholders group (water users, NGOs giving technical support, and the government) that bypassed the gram panchayat. Singh (Ibid.: 194) has argued that, for the first time, the Swajal water project demonstrated that not only could state funds be efficiently managed by village committees, but that it was also possible to recover the entire operation and maintenance cost for rural supply projects by village user committees.

Other centrally sponsored schemes of the Government of India have taken a similar route at the local level. These schemes also have been allocated substantive amount of funds (see Table 3), and have come to be known as the flagship schemes of the Government of India.

Many of these schemes are being implemented in what has come to be known as mission mode through registered societies. Implementation committees are then formed at the district and lower levels. Based on the experience of Karnataka, Chandrashekhar (2011) points out that the *society* mode of implementation has also created a parallel bureaucracy for

TABLE 3 Centrally Sponsored Schemes Lying within the Core
Functions of the Panchayats: Budget Allocation for 2007–8

	(in Rs crore)
1. Sarva Shiksha Abhiyan	10,671
2. Mid-day Meal Scheme	7,324
3. Drinking Water Mission	6,500
4. Total Sanitation Scheme	1,060
5. National Rural Health Mission	10,890
6. Integrated Child Development Scheme	4,761
7. Mahatma Gandhi National Rural Employment	
Guarantee Scheme	12,000
Total	53,206

Source: GoI 2009b.

implementing Sarva Shiksha Abhiyan, which has its
own set of problems, resulting in considerable con-
fusion regarding the performance of the tasks of the
educational bureaucracy. It is being implemented in
mission mode through registered state-level societies
which effectively bypass the decision–making process
entrusted to elected representatives.

The IRMA report (2008) points out that, in the case
of forest produce, contradictions have arisen between
the Joint Forest Management Committees and the
panchayats. The Gujarat Panchayat Act vests the forest
minor produce (except from National Parks and
Sanctuaries) on the village panchayats, and also provides
for the income earned through its sale to go to the

panchayat fund. On the other hand, through its Act of 1979, the government has vested these rights with the Gujarat State Forest Development Corporation. The result is that village panchayats have little control over minor forest produce, and are deprived of legitimate funds.

The path of establishing societies and user committees to achieve developmental goals seems to be followed in every sector. Most of these sectors are under the domain of the panchayats, and their responsibilities are getting eroded. Participation is taking a different meaning since it focuses attention on single tasks and on beneficiaries. Democratically elected panchayats are being bypassed in the process.

Caste Panchayats

To complicate matters, institutions of local governance are not confined to the formal panchayat system. Informal institutions based on caste continue to exist in most parts of the country. In a study done in three districts of Karnataka, Ananthpur (2004) provides data to show that, apart from enforcing social rules and norms, these caste panchayats also perform a range of functions such as arbitrating disputes and carrying out social functions. In many cases, instead of building inter-caste solidarity, these panchayats uphold and coerce the disadvantaged to accept social norms that are detrimental to their interests, and are instruments in keeping them under the domination of the upper castes. Newspaper reports highlight the stories of cruelty and violence meted out to dalits by these panchayats. As evidence from Rajasthan and Madhya Pradesh (Krishna 2002), Karnataka (Ananthpur 2004), and West Bengal (Gupta 2001) shows, these panchayats are surviving in many parts of the country. The activities of these panchayats in enforcing social norms influence how the dalits choose to participate in formal panchayats.

Caste panchayats continue to exist in Indian villages, parallel to the constitutionally mandated panchayats, and play a major role in regulating social behaviour. In the villages of Rajasthan, Punjab, Madhya Pradesh, Haryana, and Western Uttar Pradesh (where most of the Jats live), caste panchayats are known by their more familiar name of *khap*. A unit of khap takes care of the social affairs of the people of the same caste from several villages. Some of these panchayats can be multi-caste, but in that case they are ruled by the dominant caste. Khap panchayats are self-proclaimed arrangements of caste leaders, and enjoy legitimacy and authority among sections of their caste. They are very old social institutions, and seem to have appeared in the thirteenth and fourteenth centuries. Their survival has depended on the support that the khap leaders got from the ruling regime of the time, and even the British colonial administration incorporated them into its own revenue system.

These panchayats have been known to enforce oppressive measures against women or dalits when they transgress the norms of their traditional social behaviour. They have existed for a long time, and the colonial administration left them alone even after a modern court system was set up. It seems quite probable that Dr Ambedkar had the oppression of such panchayats in mind when he so vehemently commented against the idyllic views that the Gandhians were articulating about village life.

In recent years, honour killings have emerged as the worst manifestation of the kind of decisions that these panchayats have endorsed. They believe that individual choices in marriage are proscribed by tradition, and hence a violation needs to be avenged. When a Haryana court recently awarded capital punishment to five members of a khap for an honour killing, the community leaders were undeterred by the judgment (*The Times of India*, 1 April 2010). They are reported to have said that they would continue with the practice of settling disputes in their panchayats, irrespective of what the courts say. Similar views were echoed by the leaders of such panchayats from other states too.

Thus, caste panchayats emerge as instruments of caste dominance, enforcing traditional norms of behaviour, especially in the realm of gender and inter-caste relations. Caste panchayats have always opposed inter-caste marriages, and the Jat leadership has also fiercely put down any protest from the dalits who work as labourers in their fields. Significantly, the perpetuation of khap panchayats, as mentioned earlier, has been dependent upon the support of the state. Kumar (2012) mentions that politicians among the big Jat landlords have occupied important ministerial posts in every government in the state, and they have been eager to put a stamp of approval on the diktats of khap panchayats. In 2004, the former chief minister Om Prakash Chautala said, 'Whatever decision the panchayats take is correct.' The present Chief Minister Bhupinder Singh Hooda has said khaps are social institutions, and steps taken in a hurry to curb them will have dangerous effects on the law and order situation in the state. He has also openly opposed marriages within the same *gotra*.

Not all caste panchayats are oppressive in nature, that is, not all of them see themselves as serving solely—or mainly—to enforce traditional norms and hierarchies in relation to caste and gender. A study in Karnataka (Ananthpur 2004) found that caste panchayats not only enforce traditional rules and norms, but also perform a range of useful collective functions at the village level, often working in a consensual manner. They arbitrate a range of disputes at the village level, act as support structures by providing monetary and other assistance to people in distress, and, as found in Andhra Pradesh, often mobilize significant sums of financial and other resources for developmental projects.

Significantly, these caste panchayats are exclusive in nature and serve the interest of a particular group. The Mid-term Appraisal Report on the State of Panchayats in India (GoI 2006c) considers these caste-based bodies illegitimate—possibly illegal—and finds it disturbing that they deem themselves panchayats even as they base themselves on extremely reactionary practices—even social abuses. They give a bad name to Panchayati Raj. One also laments the fact that the retrograde actions/ decisions of these caste-based panchayats are more widely reported in the media than the regular work of the constitutionally sanctioned panchayats. Thus the government is considering ways to restrict the usage of the term panchayats only to those institutions that are mandated by the Constitution.

However, what is important to note is the coexistence of these panchayats with the formal panchayats. Democratically elected panchayats give every individual of the village the right to participate in the decision-making process by empowering even the weakest members of society—women and dalits. This right becomes partial with the continuation of arrangements that belittle the power of the weakest and encroach upon their democratic rights.

Conclusion

The governance environment of panchayats is peppered by various kinds of institutions that whittle away their sense of autonomy. The strong district administrative system, with the district collector as its head, continues. Moreover, other state departments still locate their personnel in the district, and their activities are often coordinated by the collector. Panchayats rarely have administrative control over the functionaries who are supposed to be implementing development schemes for them. Kerala appears to be an important exception to this generalization. Alternative institutions are being established to implement new programmes of rural development, and panchayats are frequently involved only in helping to execute them. Although the panchayats strive to ensure inclusive development, there is a growing sense of exclusion with user fees and other charges becoming an integral part of providing water or other resources even to the poor. Moreover, the continued existence of caste panchayats further militates against the efforts made by the constitutionally mandated panchayats to promote inclusion. The result is that panchayats frequently work in adversarial circumstances, and their leadership has to have intense devotion and commitment to succeed.

7

What does the Future Hold?

The Second Administrative Reforms Commission has subtitled its report on local governance as 'An Inspiring Journey into the Future' (GoI 2007). Indeed, it has been a long and arduous journey: from Gandhi's vision, to the constitutional deference given to panchayats by including their promotion in the Directive Principles of State Policy, and finally to the 73rd Amendment that has incorporated them into the Constitution. The preceding pages have shown how the journey progressed, what obstacles it faced, and how it has reached the stage it is in today. However, the question still remains: Has the goal of democratic decentralization and the creation of self-governing institutions at the local level been achieved? What is the hope for the future?

Undoubtedly, the 73rd Amendment has brought about a democratic revolution. There are now around 30 lakh elected representatives in panchayats, of whom around 10 lakh are women; dalits and tribals are also represented according to their proportion in the population. A recently conducted nation-wide survey of elected women representatives (GoI 2008) reveals that reservations have played a significant role in this change, since four-fifths of all representatives have been elected from reserved seats. For most of the elected women (83 per cent), it was their first entry into politics. While many women were educated at least up to middle school, about 24 per cent of them were illiterate. It is this group of women that is getting empowered, and even though a considerable number of them do not go in for re-election for various reasons, even one term in a panchayat leaves them politically aware and conscious of their rights. This has been a very significant contribution of reservations.

The entry of women and dalits into the political realm at the local level is creating an upsurge in rural society. There is violence against them by men as well as by members of the upper castes—both used to being the dominant group—providing evidence for the threat that they seem to posing to the established social system. A recent public hearing—organized by the All India Dalit Mahila Adhikar Manch—highlighted the stories of discrimination and violence against dalit women elected representatives from panchayats in Bihar, Uttar Pradesh, and Rajasthan (*The Hindu*, Delhi, 8 February 2012). There are instances in which dalit *pradhan*s have been murdered, besides other kinds of violence perpetrated on them. However, one needs to highlight the fact that such gruesome incidents have not been able to dampen the spirit of the disadvantaged groups, and there is rising political assertion on their part. As Bandopadhyay (2003) says, the new panchayats have released a new liberalizing force for dalits, women, tribals, and other socially and economically disadvantaged groups. While the entrenched groups will not yield their power easily, some political space has been provided to the socially excluded classes to assert themselves and participate in the decision-making process.

Having said this, panchayats face tremendous challenges in achieving the goals of the 73rd Amendment. Decentralization is not an easy task and, as Heller (2001: 149) points out, it requires strong, politically orchestrated action from above. Thus, it is not surprising that most of these challenges lie in the political realm. What the long journey from 1957 has shown is that there is a reluctance of the political leadership—particularly at the state level—to part with power. This reluctance is translated into the nature of the amendment and the policies adopted to further the aims of democratic decentralization. The design in the amendment consists of two kinds of provisions: those that are mandatory, and those that are discretionary. Discretionary provisions were related to the subjects listed in the Eleventh Schedule that were to be delegated to the panchayats. It was expected that the states would enact conformity legislations to establish panchayats as stipulated. These legislations incorporated the mandatory provisions which were concerned with the structure of Panchayati Raj; however, they were weak in terms of the delegation of financial and functional powers to carry out activities within the scope of the subjects delegated to them. It is for this reason that autonomy—an important attribute of a self-governing institution— has eluded the panchayats.

Several other developments have also helped to erode this concept. The reports of the State Finance

Commissions were not taken seriously, and action was not taken on them. In many cases, District Planning Committees were not established, and where they were established, they were unable to formulate plans. Panchayats were deprived of funds through schemes like the Members of Parliament Local Area Development Scheme (MPLADS), which earmarked funds to MPs for activities that were the legitimate responsibility of the panchayats. This scheme was implemented by the district administrative system. In addition, the state government's departments did not let go of their own schemes, which they implemented through their own administrative set-up at the local level. Thus, the district administrative system continued to carry on its functions as it had done in the past and perceived the panchayats as being an imposition on their structure. At best, it sought their support in implementing its projects and programmes. It is for this reason the panchayats are still regarded as additional institutions, supplementing the work of the district administration.

What further enhanced the power of the local-level administration was its role in monitoring the work of the panchayats. The functionaries of the local administration were not transferred to the panchayats, and remained part of their own hierarchies. Lacking staff, the panchayats were made dependent on the district administrative staff. In this situation, the bureaucracy is not made subordinate to democratic institutions, but is set up to regulate them.

Moreover, parallel bodies were also established in this milieu. In the changed governance styles, two kinds of things happened. One was the conceptualization of decentralization in terms of the dispersal of institutions rather than the empowerment of local democratic institutions. Decentralization was thought more in terms of de-concentration, leading to the creation of multiple bodies for delivering specific services to particular groups. Such institutions multiplied as donor agencies preferred this arrangement for providing development aid. The sprouting and flourishing of these specialized bodies can be ascribed to the scepticism of policymakers and bureaucrats regarding the abilities of the local institutions.

Thus, a contentious multiple system of governance exists at the local level, with the panchayats being ignored as far as funds, functionaries, and a clear definition of functions are concerned. The focus has shifted to the strengthening of these multiple agencies, and not on their inclusion within the purview of the panchayats, even when they are delivering the services provided for in the Fifth Schedule.

Thus, what needs to be recognized is that panchayats are being located in the broader centralized system of governance, and only hesitant steps are taken to strengthen them as self-governing institutions. Central laws continue to govern the use of local resources by the local people. Laudable objectives providing for the participation of *gram sabha*s in the use of these resources have been laid down in the panchayat legislations; however, centralized laws and the administrative system preclude them from doing so.

Notwithstanding all these weaknesses, hope lies in the democratic revolution that has taken place at local level. A very large number of elected representatives are attempting to assert their rights. They are organizing themselves to create political awareness in the socio-political system. Over 600 elected women leaders of villages across Karnataka gathered in Bangalore to launch Sugrama in May 2007. This is a unique federation to secure their rights, and further the interests of the rural communities that they serve. Lok Satta, a non-governmental organization working in Andhra Pradesh, celebrated 2005 as the year of local governments. It helped form a 'Federation for the Empowerment of Local Governments', cutting across party lines. It must be recognized that the role of civil society organizations in the institution-building of panchayats has been significant. They have, in most cases, worked with the panchayats, and created functional synergies between the panchayat and the community.

Together with this upsurge, there is another reason for optimism. There are sporadic and scattered examples of success stories. They are far and few, but they do demonstrate that there is possibility of raising resources, and utilizing them to implement schemes that benefit the people at large. There are examples of women leaders who have fought all odds and contributed to children's education, sanitation issues, and so on, and, in the process, strengthened the panchayat of which they were a part. Democratic decentralization has created spaces where the meaning of development is being contested not by leaders at the state or central level, but by the people who get directly affected. This is the significance of the democratic revolution.

Thus, there is evidence to show that decentralization has led to the deepening of democracy. No doubt, there are conflicts and contestations; but these have only helped in shaking off long held mores and beliefs in society.

Appendices

APPENDIX 1   Eleventh Schedule (Article 243G of the Constitution of India)

List of Subjects which State Legislature can Delegate
to the Panchayats

---

1. Agriculture, including agricultural extension.
2. Land improvement, implementation of land reforms, land consolidation, and soil conservation.
3. Minor irrigation, water management, and watershed development.
4. Animal husbandry, dairying, and poultry.
5. Fisheries.
6. Social forestry and farm forestry.
7. Minor forest produce.
8. Small-scale industries, including food processing industries.
9. Khadi, village, and cottage industries.
10. Rural housing.
11. Drinking water.
12. Fuel and fodder.
13. Roads, culverts, bridges, ferries, waterways, and other means of communication.

14. Rural electrification, including distribution of electricity.
15. Non-conventional energy sources.
16. Poverty alleviation programme.
17. Education, including primary and secondary schools.
18. Technical training and vocational education.
19. Adult and non-formal education.
20. Libraries.
21. Cultural activities.
22. Markets and fairs.
23. Health and sanitation, including hospitals, primary health centres, and dispensaries.
24. Family welfare.
25. Women and child development.
26. Social welfare, including welfare of the handicapped and mentally retarded.
27. Welfare of the weaker sections, and in particular, of the Scheduled Castes and the Scheduled Tribes.
28. Public distribution system.
29. Maintenance of community assets.

APPENDIX 2   Rural Population and Poverty Head-Count Ratio
by Selected States

States	Rural Population (in lakh)	Poverty Head-Count Ratio (%)
Andhra Pradesh	579.17	32.3
Bihar	799.05	55.73
Gujarat	332.76	39.1
Haryana	158.44	24.8
Karnataka	359.98	37.5
Kerala	244.81	20.2
Madhya Pradesh	476.35	53.6
Maharashtra	578.59	47.9
Odisha	324.55	60.8
Rajasthan	467.13	35.8
Tamil Nadu	334.83	37.5
Uttar Pradesh	1,416.26	42.7
West Bengal	605.33	38.2

Source: GoI 2009b.

APPENDIX 3   Status of District Planning Committees (DPCs) in States

1.	Andhra Pradesh	Not yet constituted.
2.	Arunachal Pradesh	Not yet constituted.
3.	Assam	Not yet constituted.
4.	Bihar	Constituted in all 38 districts. Chairperson of zilla parishad is chairperson of DPC.
5.	Chhattisgarh	Constituted. Minister is chairperson of DPC.
6.	Goa	Constituted. Chairperson of zilla parishad is chairperson of DPC.
7.	Gujarat	Not yet constituted.
8.	Haryana	Constituted in all 19 districts.
9.	Himachal Pradesh	Constituted. Minister is chairperson.
10.	Karnataka	Constituted. Chairperson of zilla parishad is chairperson of DPC.
11.	Kerala	Constituted. Chairperson of zilla parishad is chairperson of DPC.
12.	Madhya Pradesh	Constituted. Minister-in-charge of district is chairperson.
13.	Maharashtra	Not yet constituted.
14.	Manipur	Constituted. Chairperson of zilla parishad is chairperson of DPC.
15.	Odisha	Constituted. Minister is chairperson.
16.	Punjab	Not yet constituted.
17.	Rajasthan	Constituted. Chairperson of zilla parishad is chairperson of DPC.
18.	Tamil Nadu	Constituted. Chairperson of zilla parishad is chairperson of DPC.
19.	Uttar Pradesh	Not constituted even though the legal provision exists.

20.	West Bengal	Constituted. Chairperson of zilla parishad is chairperson of DPC.
21.	Jharkhand	Panchayat elections not yet held.
22.	Sikkim	Constituted.
23.	Uttaranchal	Not constituted even though legal provision exists.

Source: GoI 2006a.

APPENDIX 4   Number of Elected Representatives and
Percentage of Elected Women Representatives (EWR)

States		Total Elected Representatives	% age of EWRs among Total Representatives
1.	Andhra Pradesh	2,24,003	33.04
2.	Assam	25,436	38.93
3.	Bihar	1,30,091	54.12
4.	Gujarat	1,14,187	33.34
5.	Haryana	69,805	36.53
6.	Himachal Pradesh	24,581	38.86
7.	Karnataka	96,090	42.89
8.	Kerala	18,482	35.27
9.	Madhya Pradesh	3,96,516	34.35
10.	Maharashtra	2,29,740	33.33
11.	Odisha	9,24,543	36.37
12.	Punjab	90,963	34.97
13.	Rajasthan	1,20,247	35.38
14.	Tamil Nadu	1,16,488	33.79
15.	Uttar Pradesh	7,71,661	38.71
16.	West Bengal	58,828	36.29

Select Bibliography

Ananthpur, Kripa. 2004. 'Rivalry or Synergy? Formal and Informal Local Governance in Rural India', *IDS Working Paper*, 226, Institute of Development Studies, Sussex.

Babu, M. Devendra. 2009. 'Fiscal Empowerment of Panchayats in India: Real or Rhetoric?', *Working Paper*, 229, Institute of Social and Economic Change, Bangalore.

Ban, Radu and V. Rao. 2006. 'Tokenism or Agency? The Impact of Women's Reservations on Panchayats in South India', World Bank. Available at www. econ.vt.edu/seminars/.../rao-reservations-0313-wtables.pdf.

Bandopadhyay, D. 2003, 'Twelfth Finance Commission and Panchayat Finances', *Economic and Political Weekly*, XXXVIII (23): 2242–3.

Bandopadhyay, D., B. Ghosh, and Saila K. Ghosh. 2003. 'Dependency vs. Autonomy: Identity Crisis of India's Panchayats', *Economic and Political Weekly*, XXXVIII (38): 3984–91.

Bardhan, Pranab. 1996. 'Decentralized Development', *Indian Economic Review*, XXXI (2): 139–56.

Baugnet, Lucy and Girish Kumar (eds). 2011. *Indo-French Perspectives on Local Government and Democracy*. New Delhi: Manohar and Centre de Sciences Humaines.

Beher, Amitabh. 2001. 'Gram Swaraj Experiment in Direct Democracy: Madhya Pradesh', *Economic and Political Weekly*, 10 March: 819–22.

Behar, Amitabh and Yamini Aiyar. 2003. 'Networks of Panchayat Women: Civil Society Space for Political Action', *Economic and Political Weekly*, XXXVIII (47): 4936–40.

Bhattacharya, Maitree. 2002. *Panchayati Raj in West Bengal: Democratic Decentralization or Democratic Centralism*. New Delhi: Manak.

Blair, Harry. 2000. 'Participation and Accountability at the Periphery: Democratic Local Governance in Six Countries', *World Development*, 28 (1): 21–39.

Centre for Women's Development Studies (CWDS). 1999. *From Oppression to Assertion: A Study of Panchayats and Women in Madhya Pradesh, Rajasthan and Uttar Pradesh*. New Delhi: CWDS.

Chandrashekhar, Lalita. 2011. *Undermining Local Democracy: Parallel Governance in Contemporary South India*. New Delhi: Routledge.

Chaudhri, Shubham. 2007. 'What Difference Does a Constitutional Amendment Make? The 1994 Panchayati Raj Act and the Attempt to Revitalize Rural Local

Government in India', in Pranab Bardhan and Dilip Mukherjee (eds), *Decentralization and Local Governance in Developing Countries: A Comparative Perspective*, pp. 153–202. New Delhi: Oxford University Press.

Datta, Prabhat. 2009. 'Democratic Decentralization through Panchayati Raj in Contemporary India: The Changes and Challenges', South Asian and Contemporary Politics Paper No. 49, Heidelberg Papers, Heidelberg University.

Dayal, I., K. Mathur, and M. Bhattacharya. 1976. *District Administration in India*. New Delhi: Macmillan.

Deshpande, S.V. and G.B. Venkatesha Murthy. 2002. 'Pressures from Below Decentralizes Governance in Karnataka', *Economic and Political Weekly*, XXXVII (18), 4 May: 1766–7.

Dreze, Jean and Amartya Sen. 1997. *Indian Development: Selected Regional Perspectives*. New Delhi: Oxford University Press.

Fernandes, Aurleno. 2003. 'Aggrandizer Government and Local Governance', *Economic and Political Weekly*, XXXVIII (27): 2873–9.

Ford Foundation. 1959. *India's Food Crisis and Steps to Meet It*. New Delhi: Government of India.

Ghatak, Maitreesh and Maitreya Ghatak. 2002. 'Recent Reform in Panchayat System in West Bengal', *Economic and Political Weekly*, 5 January: 45–58.

Ghosh, Buddhadeb. 2000. 'Panchayati Raj: Evolution of the Concept', *Occasional Paper Series*, 25, Institute of Social Sciences, New Delhi.

Ghosh, Buddhadeb and Girish Kumar. 2003. *State Politics and Panchayats in India*. New Delhi: Manohar.

Government of India (GoI). 1978a. *Report of the Committee on Panchayati Raj Institutions* (Chairman Ashok Mehta). New Delhi: GoI.

———. 1978b. *Five Year Plan 1978–83*. New Delhi: GoI.

———. 1982. *Report of the Working Group on District Planning* (Chairman C.H.H. Rao). New Delhi: Planning Commission.

———. 1985. *Report of the Committee to Review Existing Arrangements for Rural Development and Poverty Alleviation Programmes*. New Delhi: Ministry of Rural Development.

———. 1988. *Report on Centre–State Relations* (Chairman Justice Sarkaria). New Delhi: GoI.

———. 2001a. *Report of the Expert Group*. New Delhi: Planning Commission.

———. 2001b. *Report of the Task Force Report on Panchayati Raj Institutions (PRIs)*. New Delhi: Planning Commission.

———. 2006a. *Planning at the Grassroots Level: An Action Programme for the Eleventh Five Year Plan, Report of the Expert Group*. New Delhi: Planning Commission.

———. 2006b. *Report of the Working Group on Democratic Decentralisation and PRIs*. New Delhi: Planning Commission and Ministry of Panchayati Raj.

———. 2006c. *The State of the Panchayats: A Mid-Term Review and Appraisal*. New Delhi: Ministry of Panchayati Raj.

Government of India (GoI). 2007. *Second Administrative Reforms Commission, Sixth Report—Local Governance: An Inspiring Journey into the Future*. New Delhi: GoI.

———. 2008. *Study on Elected Women Representatives in Panchayati Raj Institutions*. New Delhi: Ministry of Panchayati Raj.

———. 2009a. *Report of the Thirteenth Finance Commission*. New Delhi: Ministry of Finance.

———. 2009b. *Report of the Expert Group to Review the Methodology of Estimation of Poverty*. New Delhi: Planning Commission (Chairman: S.D. Tendulkar).

Gupta, J. 2001. 'Women, Land and Law: Dispute Resolution at the Village Level', *Occasional Paper 3*, Sachetana Information Centre, Calcutta.

Heller, Patrick. 2001. 'Moving the State: The Politics of Democratic Decentralization in Kerala, South Africa and Porto Alegre', *Politics and Society*, 29 (1), 131–63.

Heller, Patrick, K.N. Harilal, and S. Chaudhuri. 2007. 'Building Local Democracy: Evaluating the Impact of Decentralization in Kerala, India', *World Development*, 35 (4): 626–48.

Indian Institute of Public Administration (IIPA). 1997. *Legislative Status of Panchayati Raj in India*. New Delhi: IIPA.

Institute of Rural Management, Anand (IRMA). 2008. *The State of Panchayats: 2007–8*. Anand: IRMA.

Institute of Social Sciences. *Panchayati Raj Update* (monthly newsletter), New Delhi: ISS, various issues.

Isaac, T.M. Thomas and Richard W. Franke. 2001. *Local Democracy and Development: People's Campaign for Decentralised Planning in Kerala* (Revised Edition). New Delhi: Leftword Books.

Isaac, T.M. Thomas. 2001. 'Campaign for Democratic Decentralization in Kerala', *Social Scientist*, 29 (9–10): 8–47.

———. Undated. 'Decentralization in India Challenges and Opportunities', *United Nations Development Programme Discussion Paper Series*, 1, Human Resources Development Centre, New Delhi.

Jain, L.C. 1987. 'Central Planning and Karnataka's Decentralised Planning', *Mainstream*, 25 April: 15.

Jayal, Niraja G. 2003. 'Locating Gender in the Governance Discourse', in *Essays on Gender and Governance*. New Delhi: UNDP Human Resources Development Centre.

Johnson, Craig. 2003. *Decentralization in India Poverty, Politics and Panchayati Raj*. London: Overseas Development Institute.

Krishna, A. 2002. *Active Social Capital*. New York: Columbia University Press.

Kothari, Smitu. 2007. 'Challenging Centralized Governance: The Struggle for Self-Rule', in Satyajit Singh and Pradeep Sharma (eds), *Decentralization Institutions and Politics in Rural India*, pp. 278–307. New Delhi: Oxford University Press.

Kumar, Ajay. 2012. 'Khap Panchayats: A Socio-Historical Review', *Economic and Political Weekly*, XLVII (4): 59–64.

Laribi, George A. 1999. 'The New Public Management Approach and Crisis States', *UNRISD Discussion Paper*, 112, United Nations Research Institute for Social Development, Geneva.

Manning, Nick. 2001. 'The Legacy of the New Public Management in Developing Countries', *International Review of Administrative Science*, 6: 297–312.

Manor, James. 1999. *The Political Economy of Democratic Decentralization.* Washington DC: World Bank.

———. 2004. 'User Committees: A Potentially Damaging Second Wave of Decentralization', *European Journal of Development Research*, 16 (1): 192–213.

Mathew, George. 2000a. 'Panchayati Raj in India: An Overview', in *Status of Panchayati Raj in States and Union Territories of India*. New Delhi: Institute of Social Sciences and Concept Publishing Company.

———. 2000b. 'Eleventh Finance Commission on Panchayats', *The Hindu*, 16 August.

———. 2001. 'Panchayat Elections: Dismal Record', *Economic and Political Weekly*, 20 January, XXXVI (3): 183–4.

———. 2003. 'Panchayati Raj Institutions and Human Rights in India', *Economic and Political Weekly*, 38 (2): 155–62.

Mathur, Kuldeep. 2006, 'Empowering Local Government Decentralization and Governance in India', in Amitabh Kundu and Council of Social Development (eds), *India*

Social Development Report. New Delhi: Oxford University Press.

―――. 1997. 'Challenges of Decentralization: The Politics of Panchayati Raj', *Social Action*, 6 (2): 179–208.

―――. 1982. *Bureaucracy and the New Agricultural Strategy.* Delhi: Concept Publishers.

McSweeney, Brenda Gael (ed.). 2008. *Another Side of India: Gender, Culture and Development.* Paris: UNESCO.

Mundle, Sudipto. 1977. *District Planning in India.* New Delhi: Indian Institute of Public Administration.

Narayana, D. 2005. 'Institutional Change and Its Impact on the Poor and the Excluded: The Indian Decentralization Experience', Paris Working Paper No. 242, OECD Development Centre.

Oommen, M.A. 1999. *Rethinking Development: Kerala's Development Experience* (Volumes I & II). New Delhi: Concept Publishers.

Osborne, David and Ted Gaebler. 1992. *Reinventing Government: How the Entrepreneurial Spirit is Transforming the Public Sector From Schoolhouse to Statehouse, City Hall to the Pentagon.* New Delhi: Prentice Hall India.

Pal, Mahi. 2000. 'Panchayats in Fifth Scheduled Areas', *Economic and Political Weekly*, 35 (19): 1602–6.

―――. 2004. 'Panchayati Raj and Rural Governance: Experiences of a Decade', *Economic and Political Weekly*, 39 (2): 137–43.

Pal, Mahi. 2009. 'Gram Sabha Meetings in India: Processes, Outcomes and Perspectives', *Journal of Administration and Governance*, 4 (2): 91–3.

Palaniswamy, Nethra. 2010. *Sarpanch Raj: Is the President All Powerful?—The Case of Village Councils in India*. Washington DC: Development Strategy and Governance Division, International Food Policy Research Institute.

Participatory Research in Asia (PRIA). 2001. *Parallel Bodies and Panchayati Raj Institutions*. New Delhi: PRIA.

Potter, D.C. 1964. *Government of Rural India*, London: G. Bell and Sons.

Rai, Manoj, Malini Nambiar, Sohini Paul, Sangeeta U. Singh, and Satinder S. Sahni (eds). 2001. *The State of Panchayats: A Participatory Perspective*. New Delhi: PRIA and Samskriti.

Rajan, Gurukkal. 2001. 'When a Coalition of Conflicting Interests Decentralizes: A Theoretical Critique of Decentralization Politics in Kerala', *Social Scientist*, 29 (9–10): 60–70.

Ratho, Sujata. 2007. 'Tribal Welfare through Panchayats: The Experience of PESA in Orissa', *RGICS Paper*, 55, Rajiv Gandhi Institute for Contemporary Studies, New Delhi.

Rondinelli, D. and G.S. Cheema. 1983. 'Implementing Decentralization Policies: An Introduction', in Rondinelli and Cheema (eds), *Decentralization and Development: Policy Implementation in Developing Countries*. New Delhi: Sage.

156

Sahasranaman, Anand. 2012. 'Panchayat Finances and the Need for Devolutions from the State Government', *Economic and Political Weekly*, XLVII (4): 73–80.

Santha, E.K. 2002. 'Four Dalit Panchayats Prevented Again from Going to Elections', *Panchayati Raj Update*, October.

Sharma, Kumud. 1998. 'Transformative Politics: Dimensions of Women's Participation in Panchayati Raj', *India Journal of Gender Studies*, 5 (1): 23–48.

Sharma, Rashmi. 2003. 'Kerala's Decentralization Idea in Practice', *Economic and Political Weekly*, XXXVIII (36): 3832–50.

Singh, Satyajit. 2007. 'Water and Local Governments: Institutional Design, Politics, and Implementation', in Satyajit Singh and Pradeep K. Sharma (eds), *Decentralization: Institutions and Politics in Rural India*, pp. 186–222. New Delhi: Oxford University Press.

Singh, Satyajit and Pradeep K. Sharma (eds). 2007. *Decentralization: Institutions and Politics in Rural India.* New Delhi: Oxford University Press.

Slater, D. 1990. 'Territorial Power and Peripheral States: The Issue of Decentralization', *Development and Change*, 21: 501–31.

———. 2003. 'Amendment Likely on Transfer of Powers to Local Bodies', *The Hindu*, 7 December: 11.

Veron, Rene. 2001. 'The "New" Kerala Model: Lessons for Sustainable Development', *World Development*, 29 (4): 601–17.

Vyasulu, Vinod. 2003, *Panchayats, Democracy and Development* Rawat Publications, New Delhi.

World Bank. 2000. 'Decentralization', in *World Development Report 1999–2000*, pp. 107–24. Washington, D.C.: World Bank.

Index